Fr. Robert J. Kus

FLOWERS IN THE WIND 8

Still More Story-Based Homilies for Cycle B

RED LANTERN PRESS
WILMINGTON NORTH CAROLINA

www.redlanternpress.com

Books by Red Lantern Press

Journals by Fr. Robert J. Kus
- Dreams for the Vineyard: Journal of a Parish Priest - 2002
- For Where Your Treasure Is: Journal of a Parish Priest – 2003
- There Will Your Heart Be Also: Journal of a Parish Priest – 2004
- Field of Plenty: Journal of a Parish Priest – 2005
- Called to the Coast: Journal of a Parish Priest – 2006
- Then Along Came Marcelino: Journal of a Parish Priest – 2007
- Living the Dream: Journal of a Parish Priest - 2008
- A Hand to Honduras: Journal of a Parish Priest – 2009
- Beacon of Hope: Journal of a Parish Priest – 2010
- Serving God By Serving Others: Journal of a Parish Priest – 2011
- The Year of Clifton: Journal of a Parish Priest – 2012
- Basilica: Journal of a Parish Priest – 2013
- Crucifix: Journal of a Parish Priest – 2014
- Holy Doors: Journal of a Parish Priest – 2015
- Amazing!: Journal of a Parish Priest – 2016

Homily Collections by Fr. Robert J. Kus
- Flowers in the Wind 1 – Story-Based Homilies for Cycle B
- Flowers in the Wind 2 – Story-Based Homilies for Cycle C
- Flowers in the Wind 3 – Story-Based Homilies for Cycle A
- Flowers in the Wind 4 – More Story-Based Homilies for Cycle A
- Flowers in the Wind 5 – More Story-Based Homilies for Cycle B
- Flowers in the Wind 6 – More Story-Based Homilies for Cycle C
- Flowers in the Wind 7 – Still More Story-Based Homilies for Cycle A
- Flowers in the Wind 8 – Still More Story-Based Homilies for Cycle B

Nursing and Saints by Fr. Robert J. Kus
- Saintly Men of Nursing: 100 Amazing Stories

Reitocan Books by Fr. Robert J. Kus
- Reitocan Grace – Gracia Reitoqueña

ISBN-13: 978-1984367693
ISBN-10: 1984367692

Dedication

In Loving Memory of My Father

Robert T. Kus

July 4, 1918 – December 20, 2017

Acknowledgements

Many thanks go to Pat Marriott of the Basilica Shrine of St. Mary in Wilmington, N.C. who helped with the editing of these homilies.

Many thanks also go to the parishioners of both St. Catherine of Siena Parish in Wake Forest, N.C. and the Basilica Shrine of St. Mary for whom I originally created these homilies.

Thanks also go to the fine folks at CreateSpace who always do their best to assist whenever needed.

Table of Contents

Part Three – Ordinary Time

Introduction

The purpose of this book is to provide Catholic preachers a complete third collection of Sunday (and Christmas) homilies for Cycle B. Though it is designed specifically for Catholic priests and deacons, the homilies should prove useful for preachers in other mainstream Christian denominations as well.

Each homily starts with the Sunday of the Year being celebrated followed by the Scripture selection that is being discussed. This is followed by a story that appeals for people of all ages. Finally, each homily then discusses the concepts that can be gleaned from the Scripture and story and how we can apply them to our everyday lives.

Each homily takes less than eight minutes. This is especially important for preachers who are in parishes that have Masses every 90 minutes and have to get parking lots filled and emptied in a limited amount of time.

The homilies were created while I was pastor of parishes with large concentrations of children. I'm happy to say the stories make the homilies vibrant and interesting, and families love talking about the stories during the week.

Preachers may take the homilies whole, or they may tweak them to fit their specific needs.

Every effort has been made to credit the authors of each story. In the event that this was not possible, the story sources are listed as being written by "Anonymous."

Part One

❧

ADVENT &
CHRISTMAS SEASONS

Chapter 1

1st Sunday of Advent – B

The Teacup

Scripture:

- Isaiah 63: 16b-17, 19b; 64: 2-7
- Psalm 80: 2ac & 3b, 15-16, 18-19
- 1 Corinthians 1: 3-9
- Mark 13: 33-37

Today, Catholic Christians celebrate the First Sunday of Advent, the beginning of the new Church Year.

Every Advent, we look forward to hearing from the Book of Isaiah. This book has some of the most beautiful words in all of Scripture. It also has some solid messages to us. Today, for example, we hear that we are like clay, and God is the potter. In other words, we are not finished yet. Rather, we are always "under construction." But being continually formed is not always a pleasant experience, even though it is necessary. That is what the teacup in the following story found out.

There was once a couple that went shopping on their 25th wedding anniversary. One day, they saw a beautiful teacup in a little shop. Because they collected teacups as a hobby, they asked the manager to see the cup.

As soon as the manager handed them the teacup, the teacup began to talk! It told the couple that it had not always been so beautiful. In fact, it hadn't always been a teacup. Once it had just been a blob of clay. But the potter took the clay and made it what it into a beautiful teacup.

The teacup went on to say how the potter had taken the blob of clay and rolled it and put it on a spinning wheel. The teacup cried that it was dizzy, to please let it get off. The potter only said, "Not yet."

Then the potter put the teacup into a hot oven. The teacup had yelled and knocked on the door to get out, but the potter simply said, "Not yet."

When the potter took to teacup out of the oven, he put it on a shelf to cool, and the teacup was happy. However, the potter began brushing and painting the teacup, and the fumes made the teacup sick. The teacup's pleas to the potter to stop were only answered by the potter's, "Not yet."

The potter then put the teacup back into oven once again. This time, the oven was twice as hot as before. The poor little teacup cried and pleaded and begged. The potter simply said, "Not yet."

Finally, though, the potter took the teacup out of the oven and put it on a shelf to get cool. After an hour on the shelf, the potter then took the teacup and put it in front of a mirror and said, "Look at yourself."

4

At first, the teacup was astonished at beautiful it had become. The potter said, "I know that it was difficult for you when I patted you and rolled you, but if I had not done that, you would have dried up. And I know it made you dizzy when I spun you on the wheel, but if I had not done that, I could not have shaped you. And I know the oven was very uncomfortable, but without that, you would have cracked. And I had to brush and paint you so you would be hard and pretty to look at. And if I had not put you back into the oven a second time, you would not be a finished product. Now, you are done. Now you are what I have always had in mind for you to be. Now you are beautiful."

Like the teacup, we too must be formed. God shapes the lives of human beings in many ways.

For example, God gives us parents to help us to learn basic things like walking and talking. And although most parents would like to shield their children from all unpleasant things, they know that to do that would be a mistake. Children need to be able to cope with mistakes and negative things early on in life so that when they grow up they will be strong and not let the negative things of life destroy them.

God gives us teachers to expand our minds so that we can learn as much about the magnificent creation he has made.

God gives us friends and coworkers and acquaintances. They are the people who help shape us. They allow us to make mistakes, to seek forgiveness, and to start over. They are the ones who give us positive strokes when we do well, and they challenge us when we fail.

God gives us priests and other religious leaders to teach about virtues, God, Jesus, the Bible, and many other things. They give us the vision of Christ so we can put it into practice.

And finally, God gives us the poor, the strangers, the prisoners, the outcasts of society so we can put his Son's commandments into practice.

God has so many ways of shaping us, just as the potter shaped the clay into a teacup.

As we continue our life journeys this week, it would be a good idea to think of all the ways and people God is using to shape us.

And that is the good news I have for you on this First Sunday of Advent.

Story source: Anonymous, "The Teacup Story," www.creativebiblestudy.com.

Chapter 2

2nd Sunday of Advent – B

Sunshine and Prophets

Scripture:

- Isaiah 40: 1-5, 9-11
- Psalm 85: 9ab & 10, 11-12, 13-14
- 2 Peter 3: 8-14
- Mark 1: 1-8

Today Catholic Christians celebrate the Second Sunday of Advent, a day when two prophets – Isaiah and John the Baptist – remind us to prepare ourselves for the coming of the Lord.   Unfortunately, sometimes we fail to listen to the message because we have obstacles on our spiritual path that prevent us from receiving the message.   That is what happened to the man in the following story.

The story takes place in a poor section of New York City called Spanish Harlem, also called *El Barrio*.   One day, a young boy with raggedy clothes stood on a sidewalk with a small mirror in his hands.   He was holding the mirror high in the air and waving it back and forth. While he did that, he kept watching a narrow window many floors above him in one of the tenement buildings.

Suddenly a very angry-looking man came up to the young boy and roughly shook the boy's shoulders.   The man angrily demanded, "What are you up to? I imagine you are up to no good, aren't you? You street urchins are always trouble-makers."

The little boy looked up at the man's very stern and unfriendly face and said, "See that window up there, mister? Well, I have a little brother whose room is on that floor.   He is paralyzed, and the only sunlight he ever sees is what I can shine up to him with my mirror."

Wow!   What a grave mistake the man made, jumping to conclusions, seeing evil where there was great goodness and love.   We, too, sometimes jump to conclusions based on preconceived notions we have about people and our world.   Take, for example, our Scripture prophets for today.

In the first reading, we hear from Isaiah, a prophet who lived seven centuries before Jesus.   He desperately wanted people to reform their lives so they could be ready for the coming of the Messiah.   The people, though, didn't pay attention.   So Isaiah decided to wear no clothes when he went around preaching, so that people would pay attention to him.   He stayed naked for three years while delivering his message! That must have gotten their attention, don't you think?

Now, flash-forward seven centuries, and we encounter John the Baptizer.   He was a wild-looking character who was a cousin of Jesus, dressed in camel's hair and living on wild honey and locusts in the desert. What a sight he must have been!

If these two critically important prophets were alive today in the United States, what would the average Christian do? I strongly suspect that we would reject both prophets. Isaiah, for example, would be arrested for appearing naked in public, and we would probably label John the Baptizer "mentally ill" because of his wild appearance. In both cases, though, we Christians would be wrong. We would be wrong because we were focusing on the messenger rather than the message.

This is an important thing to remember: the message and the messenger are two different things. God chooses prophets and priests and writers for a purpose: to build up his Kingdom. How he chooses certain people is a mystery. The important thing is to listen to the message rather than focus on the appearance or personality of the messenger.

So what is the message that Isaiah and John the Baptizer were trying to tell us? They were telling us to make smooth the way of the Lord. They were not talking about building fine new roads; rather, they were telling us to change the landscape of our hearts and spirits. They were telling us to get rid of the obstacles in our hearts that keep us from being open to the Word of God. They were telling us to fill up the valleys and empty places in our hearts and replace them with love and compassion. They were telling us to get rid of the spiritual weeds growing in the garden of our souls, weeds such as gossip, judgmentalism, insensitivity, greed, materialism, bigotry, addictions, and other problems of the spiritual life.

But simply getting rid of the weeds is not enough. On the contrary, when we get rid of weeds, we need to replace them with flowers. Flowers of the soul include such virtues as generosity to those who have less than we do, forgiveness, joy, compassion, sensitivity, love, hope, perseverance, courage, and many others.

So, as we continue our life journeys this week, it would be good to examine our lives. What kind of obstacles do we have in our souls preventing the Lord from entering fully? What are the weeds we need to eradicate? What flowers are we planning on planting to replace these weeds?

And that is the good news I have for you on this Second Sunday of Advent.

Story source: Anonymous, "Reflect a Little Sunshine," in Brian Cavanaugh, *Sower's Seeds That Nurture Family Values: 6th Planting,* NY: Paulist Press, 2000, #62, pp. 69-70.

Chapter 3

3rd Sunday of Advent – B

A Sandpiper to Bring You Joy

<u>Scripture:</u>

- Isaiah 61: 1-2a, 10-11
- Luke 1: 46-48, 49-50, 53-54
- 1 Thessalonians 5: 16-24
- John 1: 6-8, 19-28

Today, Catholic Christians celebrate the Third Sunday of Advent. As you came into church today, you probably noted something radically different. The priest has a rose-colored vestment, the rose colored candle is lit on our Advent wreath, the sanctuary is filled with a carpet of flowers, and there are hundreds of candles burning from last night's celebration of the Patron Saint of the Americas, Our Lady of Guadalupe. It's the Third Sunday of Advent, a day sometimes referred to as *Gaudete* Sunday, the Sunday of Joy.

Joy is a virtue that we don't usually talk about too much in everyday life, but today Isaiah challenges us to consider this very Christian principle when he says, "I rejoice heartily in the Lord, in my God is the joy of my soul" (Isaiah 61: 10). And in Paul's first letter to the Thessalonians, he says, "Rejoice always" (1 Thessalonians 5: 16).

In the following story called "A Sandpiper to Bring You Joy" by Mary Sherman Hilbert, we learn how one woman came to understand how joy is a very different concept than happiness.

There was once a woman named Ruth who had recently lost her mother, and she was still depressed. One winter day, she decided to walk along a beach. As she walked along, she encountered a six-year old girl named Wendy who was building something in the sand.

Ruth stopped to greet the little girl and made small talk. Suddenly, a sandpiper glided by and Wendy said, "Oh, that's a joy. My mama says sandpipers come to bring us joy."

As Ruth left Wendy, she said to herself, "Good-bye joy. Hello pain."

During the next several weeks, Ruth continued her solitary walks along the beach where she would always encounter Wendy playing in the sand. Often, Ruth did not feel like talking as she was consumed by her depression. But she tried to stop for at least a moment to listen to Wendy. She learned that Wendy lived in a cottage where summer people usually rented, and she was very puzzled at why Wendy was not in school.

One day, when she was feeling particularly bad, she snapped at Wendy and said, "I don't want to talk today. My mother died." Ruth continued her journey alone.

12

A month later, when she returned to the beach for a walk, she did not find Wendy. She was sorry that she had snapped at the little girl the last time they had met each other, so she went to the cottage where the little girl was staying. Wendy's mother answered the door, and when she learned that the visitor was the one of whom Wendy had often spoken, she invited Ruth in.

Ruth asked Wendy's mother where Wendy was today. The mother answered, "Wendy died last week. She had been sick for some time. Maybe she didn't tell you."

Ruth was stunned at the news. Wendy's mother then said, "Wendy loved you very much, and every time you walked on the beach and said hello to her, she was filled with joy. She made this for you."

Wendy's mother then gave Ruth an envelope marked "Mrs. P." Inside was a picture Wendy had made with a yellow beach, a blue sky, and a brown bird. Underneath, Wendy had carefully printed, "A SANDPIPER TO BRING YOU JOY."

Ruth and Wendy's mother wept together, and today the picture of the little girl has a prominent place on the wall of Ruth, a woman who learned about joy that day.

For Christians, joy is a virtue. Unlike happiness that comes and goes depending on what is happening in our lives, joy is much deeper. Joy arises from a deep sense of gratitude for being part of God's creation. It is like the deep, still water in a lake. Happiness and sadness, by comparison, are like the waves on top of the lake, coming and going depending on the wind, rain, and other transitory elements.

For the Catholic Christian, joy should be second nature for us. After all, in the Catholic Christian vision, the world and people are intrinsically good because God made them. Each one of us is precious in God's sight.

Having said this, however, it is important to remember that sometimes biochemical and life events become so catastrophic for certain people that joy disappears completely from their spirits. Indeed, some people choose to end their lives of profound pain. Instead of judging such people themselves, Catholic Christians must trust God to judge and simply ask God, in his infinite love and mercy, to grant them eternal rest.

As we continue our life journeys this week, it would be good to reflect on joy. Are we glad to be part of the universe? Are we able to distinguish fleeting happiness from abiding joy?

And that is the good news I have for you on this Third Sunday of Advent.

Story source: Mary Sherman Hilbert, "A Sandpiper to Bring You Joy," in William J. Bausch, *A World of Stories for Preachers and Teachers*, Mystic, CT: Twenty Third Publications, 1998, #25, pp. 88-90.

Chapter 4

4th Sunday of Advent – B

A Passage of Many Truths

Scripture:

- 2 Samuel 7: 1-5, 8b-12, 14a, 16
- Psalm 89: 2-3, 4-5, 27 & 29
- Romans 16: 25-27
- Luke 1: 26-38

Today Catholic Christians celebrate the Fourth and final Sunday of Advent. For many of us, our minds are already into Christmas, while the Church is encouraging us to continue in Advent for a few more days.

In the Gospel reading from Luke that we encounter today (1: 26-38), we have a treasure trove of gems. In these twelve verses, we learn about several concepts important to Catholic Christians.

The story unfolds in a small town called Nazareth in Galilee. There, the Angel Gabriel appeared to a young woman, probably a teenager, named Mary. He tells her that she was to become pregnant by the power of the Holy Spirit, and that her son would be a king. The angel went on to tell her that her elderly cousin, Elizabeth, would also have a baby because with God, nothing is impossible. Mary told the angel that she was willing to do whatever it was that God wished for her.

So, what can we learn from this passage?

First, we the whole scenario of the angel coming to Mary is called the Annunciation of Jesus. We celebrate this feast day on March 25, nine months before Christmas Day. One of the most beautiful parts of this feast is Mary's response to the angel, that is, that she was willing to do whatever God wanted of her even though she did not understand what was going on. Like Mary, we too are called to this same response—to say "yes" to God even though we have no idea what the future will hold.

Second, from this passage we get the doctrine of the Immaculate Conception, the feast we just celebrated on December 8. This doctrine says that from the very moment of her conception in her mother's womb, Mary herself was free from Original Sin just like Adam and Eve at creation. This is evident from the angel's greeting, "Hail, full of grace!" After all, how can one be "full" of grace if there were sin in one's soul?

Third, we get the doctrine of the Virgin Birth from this passage. That is, Mary became pregnant from God, not another human. The doctrine of the Virgin Birth is often confused with the Immaculate Conception, but they are entirely different concepts. As an interesting aside, many religions have traditions of beings formed by the interaction of a god with a human, producing a half-god, half-human entity. In the case of Jesus, however, the Church teaches that Jesus was one hundred percent human and one hundred percent divine at the same time. This

16

Christian concept differs from those of the many religions that were common at the time of the Annunciation.

Fourth, we hear about the Holy Spirit, the Third Person of the Blessed Trinity. This concept was totally foreign to the Jewish people. As we know from history, the doctrine of the Trinity took many years to develop in the early Christian Church, with the Holy Spirit being the most difficult of the Three Persons to understand.

Fifth, from this Scripture, we hear that with God, nothing is impossible. This is indeed very good news for us. Remember when Jesus told his disciples that it is easier for a camel to go through the eye of a needle than for a rich person to get into the Kingdom of Heaven? The disciples were horrified by this concept, for that meant they were doomed. Jesus, however, reassured them by telling them though they could do nothing to "earn" salvation, all things were possible for God.

Finally, from this passage arises the Feast of Christ the King that we celebrate every year as the last Sunday in Ordinary Time. It is the idea that Christ will reign forever and ever in heaven.

So, there are a lot of things packed into these twelve short verses from the Gospel of Luke! But what do they have to do with us today?

Perhaps the most important thing we can take from the Annunciation story is that we are called to follow God's will for us no matter what. Now I'm sure some of you are saying to yourself, "Well, it would certainly be much easier if God sent the Angel Gabriel to me like he did to Mary to tell me what path I am to travel on." That is undoubtedly true, but it is quite unlikely to happen that way.

Rather, God sends each of us messages about his will for us. For example, we have various interests and desires that point the way for us. For example, my dream has always been to be a priest and to serve people. If God had wanted me to be a sports figure, he would have given me a desire to do that. We also get ideas of God's will from family, friends, and coworkers. We get ideas from school catalogues and television stories and watching others raise their children. In other words, God bombards us with so many clues for our lives that oftentimes we are overwhelmed.

The important thing is that we simply say, "Yes, God, I'll follow you no matter what. Further, I know that you will be with me on whatever path I follow. The important thing is not so much which path

17

I am on in my vocation, but rather that I follow the path in love and devotion, for I know the path will lead to you."

And that is the good news I have for you on this Fourth Sunday of Advent.

Chapter 5

Christmas - B

Misha's Gift

Scripture: (Midnight Mass)

- Isaiah 9: 1-6
- Psalm 96: 1-2a, 2b-3, 11-12, 13
- Titus 2: 11-14
- Luke 2: 1-14

Today Catholic Christians celebrate Christmas, the most magical day of the year. On behalf of all the staff and faculty of our parish, I wish you and those you love a very Merry Christmas! I pray that all your Christmas dreams come true.

Today we celebrate the birthday of the Messiah, a little boy named Jesus who was both God and human being. And on birthdays, it is customary to give presents to show our love. But what kind of present do you give to a Messiah? That is exactly what a little Russian orphan boy asked himself one Christmas. His name was Misha, and this is his story.

In 1994, two American teachers accepted an invitation from the Russian Department of Education to teach morals and ethics, based on biblical principles, in public schools and a large orphanage, which was filled with children who had been abused and abandoned.

As Christmas neared, the workers told the orphans the traditional story of Christmas. It was the very first time the orphans had ever heard the story of how Joseph and Mary went to Bethlehem, how they went to a stable because there was no room at the inn, and how the baby Jesus, born in the stable, was placed in a manger.

Throughout the story, the children and orphanage staff sat in amazement as they listened. Some sat on the edge of their stools, trying to grasp every word.

After completing the story, the teachers gave the children three small pieces of cardboard to make a simple manger. Each child was given a small paper square cut from yellow napkins. No other colored paper was available in the city.

Following instructions, the children tore the paper and carefully laid strips in the manger for straw. Small squares of flannel, cut from a worn-out nightgown, were used for the baby's blanket. A doll-like baby was cut from tan cloth the teachers had brought from the United States.

The orphans were busy making their mangers as one of the teachers walked among them to see if anyone needed any help. All went well until the teacher came to six-year-old Misha. He had already finished his project.

The teacher looked into his manger. She was startled to see not one, but two babies in the manger. Quickly the teacher called for a translator to ask Misha why there were two babies in the manger.

Crossing his arms in front of him and looking at his completed manger scene, Misha began to repeat the story very seriously. For such a young boy, who had only heard the Christmas story once, he related the happenings accurately—until he came to the part where Mary put the baby Jesus in the manger.

Then Misha started to ad-lib. He made up his own ending to the story as he said, "And when Mary laid the baby in the manger, Jesus looked at me and asked me if I had a place to stay. I told him I have no mamma and I have no papa, so I don't have any place to stay. Then Jesus told me I could stay with him. But I told him I couldn't, because I didn't have a gift to give him like everyone else did.

"But I wanted to stay with Jesus so much, so I thought about what I had that maybe I could use for a gift. I thought maybe if I kept him warm, that would be a good gift. So I asked Jesus, 'If I keep you warm, will that be a good enough gift?'

"And Jesus told me, 'If you keep me warm, that will be the best gift anybody ever gave me.' So I got into the manger, and then Jesus looked at me and told me I could stay with him—for always."

As little Misha finished his story, tears splashed down his little cheeks. Putting his hand over his face, his head dropped to the table and his shoulders shook as he sobbed and sobbed.

The little orphan boy had found someone who would never abandon nor abuse him, someone who would stay with him—*for always*.

What a beautiful lesson Misha learned that day, that Jesus would always be with him. He would never be alone again. He would never need to feel there was no one in the world that cared about him. He would always have someone to love him.

That piece of good news applies to us just as it did to the little Russian orphan boy. Jesus loves us and will always be with us. If we can just keep remembering that, we will always walk in peace.

And that is the good news I have for you on this Christmas.

Story source: Anonymous, "Misha Tells the Christmas Story," *My Favorite Christmas Stories*, December 3, 2009, World Wide Web.

Chapter 6

Holy Family – B

The Treasure

<u>Scripture:</u>

- Genesis 15: 1-6; 21: 1-3
- Psalm 105: 1-2, 3-4, 5-6, 8-9
- Hebrews 11: 8, 11-12, 17-19
- Luke 2: 22-40

Today Catholic Christians celebrate the Feast of the Holy Family, the family of Jesus, Mary, and Joseph. It is a day when all of us are called to think of our own families and the joys and challenges of family life.

In the following story from Msgr. Arthur Tonne, we learn how one man discovered how his own home, his own family, was a beautiful thing.

There was once an elderly man named George. He had never married. For almost all of his working years, George worked as a sailor traveling the oceans of the world. Because he was always at sea, he never had a home to call his own.

His nephew, Bill, had always liked his Uncle George, so when it was time for George to retire, he invited him to come and live with his wife and five children. This arrangement was beneficial not only to George, but also to Bill's family. For his part, George now had a stable roof over his head. At the same time, Bill and his family could travel the world in imagination as they listened with fascination to George's adventures sailing the world's seas.

Sometimes, when Bill listened to Uncle George' stories, he would become bored and discontented with his family life. He would think how nice it would be to roam the world free from the responsibilities he had as a husband and father. Once he even expressed this wish to his Uncle George.

One evening as Uncle George was telling one of his stories of some faraway, exotic land, he mentioned that he had a map of buried treasure. Bill was fascinated with the idea of a treasure map, so when Uncle George died a few years later, Bill went through his uncle's few belongings.

Sure enough, there was an envelope that Uncle George had addressed to him. Inside was a map, a treasure map. With his heart pounding and hands shaking, Bill studied the map very carefully, trying to figure out just where the treasure was to be found. Finally, he located the exact spot where the treasure was. It was his own home, the very spot where he was at that very moment. His Uncle George had truly left him a beautiful treasure, the realization that his own home, his own family, was a treasure.

Bill was a fortunate man. He had a family that was intact and loving. His home life was good.

But as we know, not every family is as joyful as that of the Holy Family or that of Bill's family. Sometimes, domestic violence or alcoholism or other forms of addiction rack families. Sometimes parents have fallen out of love and are staying together simply for economic security or the sake of their children. Sometimes homes have children and youth who are problematic and causing grief to their parents. Sometimes homes are plagued with poverty or ill health.

The Feast of the Holy Family does not call us to be pessimists when we look around and see problematic homes and families. On the contrary, it calls us to try to strengthen our own families.

I know there are some pessimistic people who think the family is dying. I disagree most heartily. Not only is the family not disappearing, it is thriving. In fact, today there are more types of families than in any time in the history of the world. There are nuclear families of a mom, dad, and children. There are traditional extended families, for example, where three or more generations live under one roof. There are single parent families, blended families, families with adopted children, and many other configurations. Sometimes people consider those they live with their "family" when they are far from their native land. Some people consider their church community their family. I know of monks who consider their fellow monks their family. Some of us may have more than one family—biologically based families and those of a more spiritual nature.

So don't believe the naysayers who proclaim the death of the family. The family will never die, for as long as people live, they will love. And as long as they love, they will seek to form bonds with others to share this love in an intimate way.

As we continue our life journeys this week, take some time to reflect on your own family or families. What joys and challenges does your family face? Where do you find joy and nurturing?

And that is the good news I have for you on this Feast of the Holy Family.

Story source: "Presentation" in Gerard Fuller's *Stories for all seasons,* Mystic, CT, Twenty-Third Publications/The Columbia Press, 1996, pp. 50-51.

Chapter 7

Epiphany of the Lord – B

Baboushka

Scripture:

- Isaiah 60: 1-6
- Psalm 72: 1-2, 7-8, 10-11, 12-13
- Ephesians 3: 2-3a, 5-6
- Matthew 2: 1-12

Today Catholic Christians celebrate the Feast of the Epiphany of the Lord. In the Western branch of the Catholic Church, of which we are a part, this feast is about the epiphany or "showing" of Jesus to the magi, the non-Jewish people who followed a star to the Christ Child. In the Eastern branch of the Catholic Church, the Epiphany celebrates the baptism of Jesus in the Jordan River.

The Epiphany is a very ancient feast in the Catholic Church. In fact, it is an even older feast day than Christmas. Because of its special nature, it has spawned many legends and stories to illustrate its beauty. One of my favorite stories is that of Baboushka.

Baboushka, which means "grandmother" in Russian, was an old woman who lived in a cottage by the side of the road in a forest in Russia. Because she lived alone, Baboushka developed the habit of spending most of her waking hours cleaning her cottage and keeping busy.

It was Christmas Eve, and it was very cold outside. The winds were howling, and the snow made the forest floor a look like a beautiful white carpet. Baboushka had a fire going that was making her cottage warm and cozy, and she had bread baking in the oven. She was thinking how wonderful it was that she did not have to go out in the terrible weather, when suddenly she heard a knock at her door.

When she opened it, three men entered her home. They had on robes of kings, and they carried with them gifts of gold, frankincense, and myrrh.

The one king said, "We have traveled far, Baboushka. We have been following a star to visit a Baby Prince who has been born in the West. We hear that he has come to bring love and joy into the world, and to teach all people to love one another as they love themselves. We are carrying gifts to him. Why don't you come with us, Baboushka?"

Baboushka thought of the cold winter night outside and how comfortable she was in her cottage, and said, "I'm sorry, but I'd rather stay at home. I have bread baking in the oven, and I think it's too cold outside for me."

So, the three kings left Baboushka's and went in search of the Christ Child.

Later that evening, as the darkness had fallen on the forest, Baboushka began to have second thoughts. She kept thinking that perhaps she should have gone with the Three Kings to find this newborn Prince of Peace. So, she decided that in the morning, she would set out to find the Child.

In the morning, she put on her heavy coat, took up her walking staff, and filled a basket with wooden toys, gold balls, and brilliant trinkets and left on her quest for the Christ Child. The toys were from her little son who had died many years before. Unfortunately, though, she had forgotten to ask the Three Kings exactly where the Child was located.

Baboushka walked and walked all day into the night. She walked up and down roads, through woods and fields and towns. Everywhere she went she asked, "I am going to find the Christ Child. Do you know where he is? I am bringing him some pretty toys." But nobody could tell her the way. Each person shook their head and said, "Farther on, Baboushka, farther on!"

Baboushka has never stopped looking for the Christ Child. In fact, even to this day she roams all over Russia and visits the children while they are sleeping on Epiphany Eve, sometimes called "The Twelfth Night." When she enters their bedrooms, she leaves a little toy after discovering that the sleeping child is not the Child she is looking for.

Although Baboushka usually only visits children in Russia, there are wintertime figures who bring presents to children throughout the world such as *La Befana*, the Christ Child himself, Father Christmas, Grandfather Frost, the Snow Maiden, The Three Kings, and of course St. Nicholas who is also known as Santa Claus.

Unlike Baboushka, who has never found the Christ Child, you and I do not have to worry about finding him. We have already found him. We see him when we look into the mirror or when we see our neighbor. Jesus, the Christ Child, lives in all of us, for that is what he taught us. He also reminded us that whatever we do for the least of his brethren, we do unto him.

The best gift we can give the Christ Child is not gold or frankincense or myrrh, as the Three Kings did. Rather, the only gift he wants from us is the love in our hearts. He wants us to treat every person we meet with respect, and "every person" includes us. He wants us to recognize him in others and ourselves and then act accordingly. That is why Catholic Christians feed the hungry, instruct the ignorant, give drink to the thirsty, care for the sick, visit those in prison, console those who are mourning, and the like.

Do we see Christ in ourselves? Do we see Christ in every person?

And that is the good news I have for you on this Feast of the Epiphany.

Story source: Anonymous, "Baboushka," in Tanya Gulevich (Ed.), *Encyclopedia of Christmas*, Detroit, MI, Omnigraphics, 2000, pp. 35-34.

Chapter 8

Baptism of the Lord – B

Unbaptized Arms

Scripture:

- Isaiah 55: 1-11
- Isaiah 12: 2-3, 4bcd, 5-6
- 1 John 5: 1-9
- Mark 1: 7-11

Today Catholic Christians celebrate the Feast of the Baptism of Jesus in the River Jordan. Despite the title of the feast referring only to Jesus, this story is actually about the Blessed Trinity. We see God the Holy Spirit coming down as a dove, and we hear the voice of God the Father proclaiming Jesus to be his beloved Son.

Although there are many directions in which we could go to discuss this event, today I would like to focus on our own baptism and how it calls us to be full disciples of Jesus Christ. And as always, I start with a story. Today's story is that of Otto the Conqueror.

Otto the Conqueror was a mythical ruler of long ago. He was so busy conquering new territory for his kingdom that he didn't have time to find a wife. His advisors told him he should find a wife and produce an heir. Therefore, he commanded his troops to find a nobleman's daughter for a wife.

The troops found a lovely woman named Sophia in a land across the sea. Her father, a convert to Christianity, made only one requirement: whoever married his daughter would have to be a baptized Christian. Otto agreed to that requirement and set out to marry his bride, accompanied by five hundred of his favorite warriors.

When Otto and his men arrived in Sophia's land, Otto was promptly baptized in a lake. The warriors, wanting to follow their leader, demanded that they, too, be baptized. There was one big problem, however. In those days, the Church took the command of Jesus to forgive one's enemies and not harm people very seriously. Therefore, a soldier in the early Catholic Church could not be a Christian. When the soldiers heard this news, they had grave doubts that they could be baptized.

The next morning, however, all five hundred warriors told the priest that they were ready to be baptized. All five hundred men marched out into the lake to be baptized. But before they lowered their bodies into the water, they all drew their swords and lifted them high into the air. They were quite a sight for the people on the shore who could only see five hundred dry arms and swords rising on the surface of the lake. The warriors figured they were baptized completely—except for their swords and their fighting arms.

The soldiers believed they could become "partial" Christians, giving their lives to Christ except their fighting arms, which they gave to the State.

The soldiers had a serious misconception of what it means to be baptized. They had the strange idea that only part of them could be baptized, while other parts of them were free to violate Christ's peacemaking commands. Of course you and know that this is not possible. When we are baptized, we are one hundred percent baptized. There is no such thing as being "partially baptized."

At our baptism, the Holy Spirit enters into us, permanently making us Christians, disciples of Jesus Christ. When we are baptized as Catholic Christians, we become part of the one out of every three human beings on the planet Earth who is a Christian. Immediately we have a new family of over two billion people.

But more importantly, we become anointed ministers of the Catholic Church. That means that we are called to serve others. We are official, anointed ministers. There are no exceptions.

Some people begin to demonstrate ministerial service very early in their lives. They do this in the domestic church—their home—by taking care of younger brothers or sisters, sharing toys with others, or helping their grandparents with chores.

As children grow up, they begin to have more and more opportunities to serve others. I've watched many teenagers, for example, do special tasks for elderly poor folks such as going to the store for them or mowing their lawns for free.

As adults, we have many opportunities to show how we are anointed ministers. Many young people, for example, start domestic churches. That means they get married and begin to raise families. They teach their flock, their children, how to pray, how to be grateful, how to share toys with others, how to read the Bible, how to serve others, how to perform Christian rituals such as lighting their Advent wreaths, and other things. These adults also bring their children to the second level of Church called the parish. There they receive help in raising their children in the Faith.

Opportunities to minister in the parish are numerous. In our parish, for example, we have over seventy major ministries and several minor ones. Many are open to children. In our Hispanic community, for example, it is not unusual to see children as young as eight years old serving as Ushers at weekend Masses.

Finally, Christians are called to minister to those in the workplace by helping others when they are in need of consolation, a word of encouragement, or some other type of assistance.

What kinds of ministries do you perform as an anointed minister of the Catholic Church?

And that is the good news I have for you on this Feast of the Baptism of the Lord.

Story source: Author unknown, "Unbaptized Arms," in Wayne Rice (Ed.) *More Hot Illustrations for Youth Talks.* Grand Rapids, Michigan: Youth Specialties/Zondervan, 1995, pp. 169-170.

Part Two

❧

LENT &

EASTER SEASONS

Chapter 9

1st Sunday of Lent – B

The Drunk Driver

Scripture:

- Genesis 9: 8-15
- Psalm 25 4-5ab, 6 & 7bc, 8-9
- 1 Peter 3: 18-22
- Mark 1: 12-15

Today, Catholic Christians celebrate the First Sunday of Lent.

On this day, we hear Jesus telling the people of Galilee, "This is the time of fulfillment. The kingdom of God is at hand. Repent, and believe in the gospel" (Mark 1: 15).

That admonition is just as relevant to us today as it was two thousand years ago. Many people refuse to repent, but some, like the young man in this story, did change his life for the better.

The story takes place in a small town in Vermont far from any large city. This town had only one physician and one nurse, both of whom everyone in the town loved very much. Late one night, as the physician was driving home from delivering a baby, a drunk driver coming the other way on a dark country road crashed into the physician's car.

The driver of the car was a young man that nobody in the town liked very much. He was a very intelligent young man, but he was lazy. He had gone away to college, but he quit school and returned to the little town. There he spent his days sleeping and loafing, and he spent his evenings and nights drinking and racing his car while everyone was trying to sleep. This night, as usual, he was driving drunk.

A farmer heard the crash and rushed to the accident. He called for the nurse to come to the accident scene. After determining that both the physician and young man were both hurt very badly, and that she would not be able to help both of them quickly enough, she went to help the physician. He, however, whispered, "No. Help the young man first."

The nurse was astonished and exclaimed, "That drunk? You are the one we need. You're the only physician in our town!"

With the last bit of strength he had, the physician insisted, "I'm an old man and have had a long and good life. His is just beginning. Help him first."

So, the nurse did help the young man. The next morning, when the nurse learned that the physician had died and the young man was still alive, she screamed at the young man, "See what you've done! You've killed the best person in the whole town. You are nothing but a drunk! You are the one that should be dead, not him! He died so you could live. Now our town has no physician. What are you going to do about that?"

That day, the young man began to turn his life around. Instead of being permanently scared and destroyed by the experience, he went back to school and studied medicine. After graduation and completing his residency, he came back to the little Vermont town and became its new physician. As the years went on, the people of that little town came to love this man just as they had loved the physician who had given up his life.

The story of the drunk driver is a story of repentance. This is what Jesus was trying to tell us today. We need to turn our life around, to change direction, when we are going astray.

This is the message we heard this past week at our Ash Wednesday services. As the ministers made a Sign of the Cross with ashes on our foreheads, they said, "Turn away from sin and be faithful to the Gospel."

Most of us, fortunately, have not had such a life-changing and dramatic experience as the young drunk driver in the story. Most of us have not killed another human being by our behavior. Nevertheless, all adults need to change direction in some areas of their lives.

Perhaps, for example, we destroy others' reputations with our gossip. Perhaps we carry around anger or grudges in our hearts. Maybe we are stingy with our time, talent, or treasure, contrary to the teaching of Jesus. Maybe we could more generously give of ourselves by visiting the sick, writing a friendly letter to someone in prison, consoling those who are in sorrow, giving alms for the poor, or showing our generosity in other ways.

Perhaps we violate the third part of the triple love commandment of Jesus Christ by not loving ourselves. Maybe we harm ourselves by overeating, not exercising, not taking medicines correctly, failing to treat negative addictions, refusing to get physical checkups, or failing to get adequate rest.

Needless to say, all of us have work to do. Jesus' call to "Repent!" is meant for each and every one us. Lent is an ideal time to strive for repentance as we get ourselves ready to renew our baptismal promises at Easter.

What kind of repentance do you need to work on? Do you have a plan for this Lent?

And that is the good news I have for you on this First Sunday of Lent.

Story source: Anonymous, "The Drunk Driver Story," in Thomas W. Goodhue (Ed.), *Sharing the Good News with Children: Stories for the Common Lectionary.* Cincinnati, Ohio: St. Anthony Messenger Press, 1992, p. 141.

Chapter 10

2nd Sunday of Lent – B

The Circus

Scripture:

- Genesis 22: 1-2, 9a, 10-13, 15-18
- Psalm 116: 10 & 15, 16-17, 18-19
- Romans 8: 31b-34
- Mark 9: 2-10

Today, Catholic Christians celebrate the Transfiguration of Jesus.

In the Transfiguration story, Jesus takes three of his apostles – Peter, James, and John – up on a mountain to pray. The disciples get distracted when Moses and Elijah appear with Jesus. Instead of keeping their focus on Jesus, they begin to treat all three men as equals.

Getting sidetracked is easy to do, especially if we don't have a clear understanding of what we are supposed to be focusing on. That is what happed to the poor little boy in the following story.

There was a little boy who lived far out in the country in the early twentieth century. One day, he saw a poster at his school saying that a traveling circus was coming to town the following Saturday.

He raced home to ask his dad if he could go. Though the family was very poor, the father saw how excited his son was about the circus. So, he said, "If you do your Saturday chores ahead of time, I'll give you some money to go to the circus."

The little boy was ecstatic with joy, for he had never been to a circus before. On Saturday, he was up before the rooster crowed and did his chores in record time. Then he stood dressed in his Sunday-best clothes in front of his father at the breakfast table. His father reached into his old overalls and pulled out a dollar bill and gave it to his son. This was the most money the little boy had ever seen.

The boy was so excited that his feet hardly touched the ground as he ran to the village. When he got to the village, he noticed all the people lined up and down the street. He joined them just as the beginning of the circus parade began marching down the street.

This was the most spectacular thing the little boy had ever seen. There were tigers and apes in cages and bands and little people and an elephant and all the things that make up a fine circus. At the very end of the parade was a clown complete with floppy shoes and baggy pants and a brightly painted face. As the clown passed the little boy, the boy reached into his pocket, ran up to the clown, and handed his precious dollar to the clown. He then turned around and made his way home.

The poor little boy thought that the parade was the circus. All he had seen, though, was the preview and missed the wonderful performances that were to come in the circus tent.

A similar thing happened to Peter, James and John. Here they were with Jesus when Moses and Elijah showed up and began talking with Jesus. The disciples wanted to make tents in honor of all three. But just as they were about to do so, a cloud came over them and a voice said, "This is my Son, my beloved. Listen to him." Suddenly, Moses and Elijah disappeared, leaving the disciples alone with Jesus once again.

What does this all mean? Well, the dazzling white clothes of Jesus symbolize his divinity. Moses symbolizes the Old Testament Law, while Elijah symbolizes the Old Testament Prophets. In Scripture, a cloud descending on people refers to God the Father giving a direct message from heaven. And when Moses and Elijah disappear, we learn that the Old Testament Law and Prophets have been fulfilled. Now all we need is Jesus. Jesus is the fulfillment of the Law and Prophets of the Old Testament. He is the one we must keep our eyes on. He is the one to follow. Thus, when Jesus taught us the triple love commandment—to love God, our neighbor, as we love ourselves—he told us that this was the summary of all the law and the prophets.

As Catholic Christians, we believe that Jesus is the head of our Church. He is the one to follow, and he is always with us.

The Church fathers, at the Second Vatican Council from 1962 to 1965, told us that Jesus Christ is really present at every Eucharist (Mass) in four distinct ways.

First, he is really present in the assembly. The assembly refers to everyone who comes to celebrate Mass and sits in the pews.

Second, he is really present in the proclaimed Sacred Scriptures. Thus, we see the profound importance that the Ministry of Lectors has in our Faith.

Third, Jesus is really present in the presider, the priest. Thus, the priest represents Christ as the head of the assembly at Eucharist. Thus, he does not say "This is Jesus' body" or "This is Jesus' blood," but rather, he says, "This is my body" and "This is my blood."

And finally, Jesus is really present in the consecrated elements of bread and wine that we commonly refer to as "Communion."

It's easy to get sidetracked, to turn our attention to things other than Jesus. But today we learn that Jesus is all we need. He is the ultimate source of our Faith. All else is secondary.

And that is the good news I have for you on this Second Sunday of Lent.

Story source: Anonymous, "Transfiguration," in Gerard Fuller (Ed.), *Stories for All Seasons*. Mystic, CT: Twenty-Third Publications/The Columbia Press, 1996, pp. 54-55.

Chapter 11

3rd Sunday of Lent – B

Love and the Cabbie

<u>Scripture:</u>

- Exodus 20: 1-17
- Psalm 19: 8, 9, 10, 11
- 1 Corinthians 1: 22-25
- John 2: 13-25

Today Catholic Christians celebrate the Third Sunday of Lent.

On this day, we hear about the Decalogue in the Book of Exodus (20: 1-17). Most people today refer to the Decalogue as "The Ten Commandments." These were a part of more than six hundred laws of the Old Testament given to the Hebrew people to follow. Many Catholic Christians use these commandments in examining their consciences as the make their Lenten Reconciliations.

We know, though, that Jesus gave us many more commandments to follow, commandments such as forgiving those who harm us. Jesus realized how confusing all these laws or commandments could be to people, so he simplified it by giving us the triple love command, a synthesis of all the Old Testament law and prophets: love God, love your neighbor, as you love yourself.

Many Catholic Christians don't seem to grasp this. They don't know how to put love into practice into everyday life. Therefore, they err by "omission," that is, they fail to do good, instead of by "commission," deliberately doing bad.

In the following story, a man I'll call "Pablo," understood what Jesus was talking about.

Art Buchwald was an American humorist who died in 2007. One day, he was riding in a taxicab in New York City with his friend Pablo. When they got out of the cab, Pablo told the cab driver, "Thank you for the ride. You did a super job of driving this cab!"

The cab driver was stunned for a moment and then replied, "Are you a wise guy or something?"

"No," said Pablo. "I'm serious. I admire the way you keep cool in heavy traffic. Not many cab drivers are able to do that. I'm glad I rode in your cab today!"

The cab driver drove off. Art Buchwald asked his friend about the interchange. Pablo replied, "I'm trying to bring love back to New York City. I believe it is the only thing that can save the city."

Art told Pablo that though this was a noble thing, one man could not make much of a difference. But Pablo disagreed. He pointed out that his compliments would not just affect one man. He pointed out by being nice to the cab driver, it perhaps made the driver's day brighter. If the driver than had twenty fares that day, he might be nicer to the people in his cab. Those people will in turn be nicer to their employees, shopkeepers, waiters, or even their families. Eventually, Pablo's good will toward the cab driver could spread to at least a thousand people.

When Art said, "Well, all that depends on the cab driver passing on your goodwill to others," Pablo replied, "Maybe he won't. But if I say something nice to ten people, and only three pass it along, I can affect three thousand people today in a positive way."

Art turned to Pablo and said, "I think you're crazy."

Pablo turned to Art and said, "That just shows you how cynical you have become."

As they walked along the city streets, Pablo went out of his way to give a compliment to the mail carrier and some workmen who were sitting having their lunch. Art said, "I think you are wasting your time, Pablo."

"On the contrary," replied Pablo, "when those workers digest my words, they'll feel better about what they are doing and somehow the city will benefit."

"But you can't do this alone," replied Art. "You're just one man."

"True," replied Pablo, "but I plan on enlisting others in my campaign to spread love."

As they continued to walk down the street, Pablo smiled warmly at a very plain-looking woman and gave a cheery "hello." Art said to Pablo, "You just smiled and were polite to a very plain-looking woman."

"Yes, I know," said Pablo. "And if she is a schoolteacher, her class is going to be in for one fantastic day!"

This is a terrific story because it shows us so vividly that we can put Christ's love into practice in everyday life. And you don't have to go the streets of New York. You can do it wherever you live with whomever you meet.

So, in case you can't think of anything you did wrong since you last celebrated Reconciliation, you might examine your life and think of all your many missed opportunities to put Christ's triple love commandment into practice. If you are like most people, that ought to keep you busy a long time.

And that is the good news I have for you on this Third Sunday of Lent.

Story source: Polich, Laurie, "Love and the Cabbie," in Wayne Rice (Ed.), *More hot Illustrations for Youth Talks,* Grand Rapids, MI: Youth Specialties Books/Zondervan Publishing House, 1995, pp. 111-113.

Chapter 12

4th Sunday of Lent – B

Salvation and the Supermarket

Scripture:

- 2 Chronicles 36: 14-16, 19-23
- Psalm 137: 1-2, 3, 4-5, 6
- Ephesians 2: 4-10
- John 3: 14-21

Today, Catholic Christians celebrate the Fourth Sunday of Lent. This is one of the two Sundays of the year when the priest may wear rose-colored vestments, indicating joy.

And today we indeed hear joyful news about salvation when we read, "For God so loved the world that he gave his only Son, so that everyone who believes in him might not perish but might have eternal life. For God did not send his Son into the world to condemn the world, but that the world might be saved through him" (John 3: 16-17). This is indeed joyful news, for many people wonder if they will go to heaven when they die. They wonder how to get to heaven. Is salvation a pure gift, or is it something we must earn?

The following story gives us a clue about salvation from a Catholic Christian perspective.

Once there was a supermarket sweepstakes in which five finalists each won a fifteen-minute shopping spree. The people were allowed to go through the store and put whatever they wanted into their shopping carts. At the end of fifteen minutes, the cashier would ring up the contents of each shopping cart. The person with the highest total would win the sweepstakes.

The finalists dashed through the store as fast as their legs could carry them. They grabbed the most expensive items they could find and crashed into each other and the counters. Basically, they raced around the store as though their lives depended on it.

There was one young man, however, who was not dashing around the store like the others. He was very calm, casually choosing items from the shelves and putting them in his cart. One of the finalists shouted as him as she sped by with her shopping cart, "Why are you going so slowly and not rushing like everyone else?"

The young man smiled and said, "Well, it's because my father owns the store."

I love this story because it calls to mind the great concern we all have with what will happen to us in the afterlife. As Christians, we realize that "our Father" indeed "owns the store," the "store" being "heaven." Will not his children go to heaven?

For the two thousand years of Christianity, Christians have argued and debated over who will go to heaven.

50

On the one side are fundamentalists who believe that only a very select crowd will get to heaven. They, of course, are convinced they are part of that crowd. For fundamentalists, Christ's dying on the cross was only effective for a few people. Furthermore, they argue, to make the Calvary event effective, they themselves to work to release its graces. The work they have to do is this: First, they have to accept Jesus as their personal Savior; and second, they have to tell others about how they have been saved. If they don't do these two actions, the effects of Calvary will not be released.

Some Christians believe that they have to "earn" salvation by good works. Instead of having faith in God, they are like the fundamentalists who believe they have the power to make or break their path to salvation.

The third view, the Catholic Christian view, is that salvation is not something we earn. Rather, it is a pure gift from God. Further, the Catholic Christian view, in stark contrast to the fundamentalist notion, is that Jesus' dying on the cross was powerful in and of itself. It does not need our work to make it powerful or effective. We do good works because Jesus commanded us to do so. Further, in the Catholic Christian view of salvation, we believe that God's will is for all people to be saved because that is why we were created. Catholic Christians further believe that God's mercy and love have no limits. And finally, Catholic Christians believe that "with God, all things are possible." Therefore, at each Eucharist, Catholic Christians ask God for the salvation of all humanity.

Does this mean, therefore, that God will grant salvation to all humanity just because Catholic Christians ask it? No, that is not what we are saying. We don't know the mind of God. Our prayer expresses our joyful hope that indeed, all will be saved through the mercy and love of God.

On the other hand, does this mean there is no such thing as "hell," a place eternally removed from God? No. But in the two thousand years of Catholic Christianity, the Church has never declared that there is a human being in a state called hell, though the Church has always held that a person could conceivably go to such a state. The only "state" where the Church has definitively stated certain persons have gone in the afterlife is heaven.

51

So, who is going to be saved? That is God's job to determine, not ours. Our job is to love God, love our neighbors, as we love ourselves. That is what Jesus taught us. And part of loving others is to pray daily for the salvation of all humanity.

Do I believe that all persons will be saved? I am like the late Pope John Paul II who believed that all would be saved. He believed this not as pope, but as a Catholic Christian. In other words, it was his personal hope and belief, not something he taught as pope. But like that pope, I am very clear that this is only my prayer, my hope. Only God knows if the prayers of John Paul II and me will become a reality in the life hereafter.

And that is the good news I have for you on this Fourth Sunday of Lent.

Story source: Anonymous, "Supermarket Sweepstakes," in Brian Cavanaugh (Ed.), *Sower's Seeds Aplenty: Fourth Planting,* New York: Paulist Press, 1996, #51, p. 38.

Chapter 13

5th Sunday of Lent – B

St. Peter Chanel

Scripture:

- Jeremiah 31: 31-34
- Psalm 51: 3-4, 12-13, 14-15
- Hebrews 5: 7-9
- John 12: 20-33

Today, Catholic Christians celebrate the Fifth Sunday of Lent.

On this day, we hear Jesus talking about death and resurrection. He says in the Gospel of John, "The hour has come for the Son of Man to be glorified. Amen, amen, I say to you, unless a grain of wheat falls to the ground and dies, it remains just a grain of wheat; but if it dies, it produces much fruit. Whoever loves his life loses it, and whoever hates his life in this world will preserve it for eternal life" (John 12: 23-25).

What Jesus meant was not that we should literally hate human life, nor should we hate each other or ourselves. On the contrary, we should love life and our neighbors and ourselves. That is part of the triple love command he taught us. That is the very foundation of what Jesus stood for. What he meant was that we should put God before all and not fall in love with life in the world, with things like money or power or prestige. Some spiritual masters call this being "in the world but not of the world."

However, there have been plenty of people that God has put in the world to show how an individual who dies can be like the grain of wheat that dies and then produces much fruit. One such person was St. Peter Chanel.

Peter was born in France and lived from 1803 to 1841. Because of Peter's intelligence and piety, the local priest of his town took a keen interest in Peter. He nurtured his elementary education and saw to it that he entered the diocesan seminary. In the seminary, both faculty and students loved Peter.

When Peter was ordained, he was assigned to a rundown country parish. In the three years he was there, he revitalized it and made it thrive and flourish.

Though Fr. Chanel was an excellent parish priest, his heart and mind were set on being a foreign missionary. Therefore, in 1831 he joined a new religious order called the Society of Mary (Marists) that concentrated on both domestic and foreign missionary work.

He was understandably sad, though, to find that his first assignment in this missionary order would be to teach at the local seminary. However, he did his best as a seminary instructor for the next five years.

Then, in 1836, Fr. Peter was assigned to be the Superior of a small band of missionaries assigned to New Hebrides in the Pacific Ocean. It took ten months for the little band to reach their destination in this sprawling French/English colony. When they got there, the band broke up, each group going to a different island. Fr. Peter went with a lay brother and a lay Englishman to the Island of Futuna.

When Fr. Peter and his two companions first arrived on the island, the king and people greeted them warmly. The king had recently banned the practice of cannibalism among the people.

Fr. Peter and his companions got busy and learned the language of the people, and they gained the people's confidence. This made the king jealous. He was further concerned that if the people became Christians, he would lose some of his prerogatives as king.

Fr. Peter nevertheless continued to do his missionary work, but he did not seem very successful. He had trouble with the whalers and traders who came to the island. He faced hostility from warring natives. He baptized only a few people, and only a few more were studying to become baptized. But despite all his difficulties, he worked patiently and continued to have a gentle spirit.

Then one day, the king's son asked to be baptized. This made the king so angry that he sent a group of warriors to kill Fr. Peter. On April 28, 1841, three years after his arrival on the Island of Futuna, they clubbed Fr. Peter to death and then cut up his body into pieces. With his death, Fr. Peter Chanel became the "proto" or "first" martyr of Oceania.

The story, though, did not end with Fr. Peter's death. Rather, within two years, the whole island became Catholic and has continued to treasure the Faith even to this day.

Peter was proclaimed a Saint in 1954. St. Peter Chanel is the Patron Saint of Oceania.

Few if any of us will ever be given the privilege of being a martyr. All of us, though, are called to be like the grain of wheat that dies so we can be fruitful. We do this by refusing to be enslaved by the glittering things of the world: money, power, prestige, or possessions. Instead, we are called to fall in love with serving the Lord by serving each other. Then the fruits of our lives will become many.

And that is the good news I have for you on this Fifth Sunday of Lent.

Story source: "St. Peter Chanel," in Peter Doyle (Revision Editor), *Butler's Lives of the Saints New Full Edition – April*, Collegeville, MN: Burns & Oats/The Liturgical Press, 1999, pp. 195-197.

Chapter 14

Palm Sunday of the Passion of the Lord – B

Holy Week

Scripture:

- Isaiah 50: 4-7
- Psalm 22: 8-9, 17-18a, 19-20, 23-24
- Philippians 2: 6-11
- Mark 14: 1 – 15: 47

Today Catholic Christians celebrate Palm Sunday of the Lord's Passion – more commonly known simply as Palm Sunday. This day marks the beginning of Holy Week, the most special week of the year for Christians.

On this day, we read about how the people gave Jesus a great welcome into Jerusalem (Mark 11: 1-10). Later, however, we learn how they turned against him when we hear the Passion according to St. Mark (14: 1 – 15: 47).

This week, the bishop and priests of each diocese gather to celebrate the annual Chrism Mass. At that Mass, the clergy will renew their priestly promises, and they will bless the three oils that will go to each parish for the coming year. The oils will be used to celebrate various sacraments in the parishes.

On Holy Thursday evening, we will begin a special Mass called the Mass of the Lord's Supper. As that Mass begins, the Season of Lent officially ends for Catholic Christians, and we enter a three-day Season called Triduum. At this Mass, the people will bring the three oils blessed at the Chrism Mass to the priest, and the priest will wash the feet of some people just as Jesus washed the feet of the Twelve Apostles. The washing of the feet symbolizes the new form of leadership Jesus gave to his disciples, that is, to be the leader, one must be the servant of all. We call this the "servant-leader" model of leadership.

On Good Friday, we commemorate Jesus' Passion and Death with the reading of the passion, veneration of the cross, and a Communion Service. In many parishes, such as our own, members of the Hispanic community will put on a live *Via Crucis* (Way of the Cross) outdoors.

On Holy Saturday evening, Catholic Christians celebrate the most elaborate ritual of the year – the Easter Vigil ceremonies. At this time, in addition to celebrating Mass, we also have the Blessing of the New Fire, Blessing of the New Water, and Blessing of the Easter Candle; and most importantly, we will celebrate the Sacraments of Initiation for many catechumens.

On Easter Sunday, we will have seven Masses.

Try to attend as many of these special events as possible. You will be richly blessed.

And that is the good news I have for you on this Palm Sunday.

Chapter 15

Easter – B

The Apostle

Scripture:

- Acts 10: 34a, 37-43
- Psalm 118: 1-2, 16-17, 22-23
- 1 Corinthians 5: 6b-8
- John 20: 1-9

Today Catholic Christians celebrate the most important feast of the Catholic Church, Easter - the Resurrection of Jesus Christ. Easter commemorates the day Jesus rose from the dead, never to die again. It is the victory of light over darkness, of good over evil, and of life over death. It is truly a "good news" story, a fantastic story, the very finest Christian story.

On behalf of the staff and faculty of our parish, I wish you and those you love a most Blessed Easter. I pray that the Holy Spirit will touch your hearts in a very special way this sacred season and give you renewed faith, hope, love, and joy.

On this Feast of the Resurrection, I call to mind one of my favorite movies and its significance for us as "Easter people."

The movie is The Apostle, starring Robert Duvall, and it concerns the life of a Holiness-Pentecostal preacher who called himself the Apostle E.F.

When he was a little boy, his African-American caretaker took him to her little Pentecostal church in Texas. There he was touched by the Lord, and by the time he was 12 years old, he was preaching to the church.

When he grew up, he had a very successful Pentecostal church in Texas, but he lost it one day to his enemies. In a fit of anger, after losing his wife and children to the youth minister in his church, he struck the youth minister with a baseball bat and killed him.

He immediately ran away and eventually found himself in a small Louisiana town, where he teamed up with an African-American preacher named Rev. C. Charles Blackwell. Together, they resurrected a little abandoned church with paint and lots of love.

The little church, that the Apostle E.F. called "The One Way Road to Heaven," rapidly came to life. Soon it was filled with shouts of joy to the Lord, clapping, singing, dancing, and the wonderful preaching of the Apostle E.F. People gave their lives to Jesus.

Inevitably, the Apostle E.F. was eventually caught by the police and sent to prison for murdering the youth director of his old church. The final scene in the movie shows the Apostle E.F. working with fellow inmates clearing brush from the side of the road. Even then, he was leading the others in song in praising Jesus Christ.

But what does the movie have to do with us today, and what does it have to do with the theme of "resurrection" or "new beginnings?" Let's take a look.

First, we learn that God can work through any human being. It was true that the Apostle E.F. killed a man and was a womanizer and had a bad temper, but God chose him as his instrument. God was able to take E.F.'s talents and use them to spread the message of love and bring souls to Jesus Christ. We learn, therefore, that it is the message, not the messenger that is important for us. All Christians, by virtue of their baptism, are called to be messengers of God. Some, like priests, are ordained to spread the word through preaching. Others are called to spread the word merely by living good lives.

Second, any time is "resurrection time," whether we are resurrecting a building or a life. Every adult human being on the planet has a need to change and grow. There are no exceptions. Perhaps we need to rid our lives of fear, or greed, or credit card irresponsibility, or infidelity, or anger, or lack of forgiveness, or addiction, or overeating, or whatever. The Apostle E.F., although he kept making mistakes in his life, never stopped trying to better himself, never stopped trying to be more like Christ.

Third, we are all on a journey together. Every life has dark moments and tough times. Just because others seem to have no problems, don't be fooled. Everyone has problems. We are called to help each other make the burden lighter. A simple smile or a friendly greeting can make a world of difference to someone whose spirits are down.

Fourth, we see in the movie that no matter what happened to the Apostle E.F.—losing his first church, losing his wife and kids to divorce, ending up in prison—the message of the Resurrection was present in his life. In other words, we see that the power of light is stronger than the power of darkness. The power of goodness is stronger than the power of evil. The power of life is stronger than the power of death. And the power of love is stronger than the power of hate.

What kind of new growth are you called to on this Easter Sunday?

And that is the good news I have for you on this Feast of the Resurrection.

Story source: *The Apostle*, Butcher's Run Films, 1997.

Chapter 16

2nd Sunday of Easter - B

Tent of Refuge

Scripture:

- Acts 4: 32-35
- Psalm 118: 2-4, 13-15, 22-24
- 1 John 5: 1-6
- John 20: 19-31

Today Catholic Christians celebrate the Second Sunday of Easter. Since the Year 2000, Catholic Christians have celebrated this Sunday as "Divine Mercy Sunday." It is a day when we thank God for his boundless mercy, and we vow to be merciful toward others, as we would like God to be merciful toward us.

In the following story, we see an incredibly beautiful example of a how one old man showed mercy when he so easily could have shown vengeance.

There was once a young Bedouin man by the name of Abdul who lived in the kingdom of Jordan long ago. One day, he got into a fight with another young man. In the midst of the fight, Abdul pulled out a knife and plunged it into the other young man's chest, killing him instantly.

When Abdul realized what he had done, he fled in fear across the desert to avoid retribution by the other man's relatives. Abdul's destination was what was called a "tent of refuge," a sanctuary created by Bedouin law that protected those who killed others unintentionally or in the heat of anger.

Finally, Abdul reached the "tent of refuge." He flung himself at the feet of the sheik—the leader of the tribe—by the name of Rashid. Young Abdul pleaded with Rashid: "I have killed another young man in a fit of anger. I beg of you to give me protection. I seek the refuge of your tent."

The wise old Rashid took pity on the young man and said, "If God wills it, I grant it to you as long as you remain here with us."

A few days later, the avenging relatives tracked Abdul to the tent of refuge. They described Abdul to Sheik Rashid and said, "Have you seen this man? Is he here? We want him."

Sheik Rashid replied, "Yes, he is here. But you may not have him. This is a tent of refuge, a place of sanctuary. As long as he is with me, he is safe."

The relatives of the slain young man became intensely angry. They demanded that Sheik Rashid turn over Abdul so they could kill him. Sheik Rashid, however, would not yield.

Finally, the avenging relatives of the slain young man said, "But the young man that Abdul killed was your grandson!"

The old sheik became very silent. No one dared to speak. Then, with tears running down his face, Sheik Rashid stood up and asked very slowly, "My only grandson—he is dead?"

"Yes," the relatives replied, "he is dead. Abdul killed him."

"Well," said the sheik, "because I no longer have a grandson, I will adopt Abdul as my new grandson. He is forgiven, and he will live with me as my own grandson. Go now; the case is finished."

What an astonishing story of forgiveness and mercy this is. Perhaps you would ask, "If I were the sheik, would I have been so quick to offer forgiveness? Would I be so quick to offer mercy?"

From the Catholic Christian perspective, mercy is one of the most precious qualities of God. In fact, we continually ask God for mercy, for not punishing us for the things we do wrong. In fact, we treasure divine mercy so much, that at every Eucharist we ask God to shower his mercy on all humanity so that every single human being who ever lived, is living, and ever will live will spend eternity with him.

But being grateful for God's mercy, and asking God for mercy, is not enough. On the contrary, each of us is called to be "God-like," to follow his example. We are called to be merciful, just as God is merciful.

Mercy, though, has two different meanings. "Mercy," when we speak of "divine mercy," means restraint from punishment. We are called by God to show that type of mercy by such endeavors as fighting against capital punishment and fighting against automatic sentences of life imprisonment.

The more common type of mercy to which Catholic Christians are called is defined as "active compassion toward another person in unfortunate circumstances; an essential form of charity." We perform corporal works of mercy when we care for the physical needs of others, and we perform spiritual works of mercy when we care for the psychological and spiritual needs of others.

As we continue our life journeys this week, let's take some time to reflect on how we practice mercy. How quick are we to forgive? How quick are we to grant mercy to others?

And that is the good news I have for you on this Second Sunday of Easter.

Story source: Walter J. Burgart, "Tent of Refuge," in Brian Cavanaugh (Ed.) *Sower's Seeds that Nurture Family Values, Sixth Planting*, New York, Paulist Press, 2000, #93, pp. 98-99.

Chapter 17

3rd Sunday of Easter – B

The Prince of Granada

Scripture:

- Acts 3: 13-15, 17-19
- Psalm 4: 2, 4, 7b-8a, 9
- 1 John 2: 1-5a
- Luke 24: 35-48

In the Gospel reading we have today from Luke on this Third Sunday of Easter, Jesus appears to his disciples after his resurrection. He then begins to do what today is commonly known as "Bible Studies." Specifically, he shows them how things written in the Old Testament Scripture passages referred to him. He tells them: "Thus it is written that the Christ would suffer and rise from the dead on the third day and that repentance, for the forgiveness of sins, would be preached in his name to all the nations, beginning from Jerusalem" (Luke 24: 46-47).

Bible Studies is a fine endeavor, but in and of itself it is insufficient. For if we do not put what we learn into practice in our daily lives, it is simply an academic exercise. That is exactly what we see in the following story about a prince who spent much of his life in prison.

Many centuries ago, man, the Prince of Granada, a young man who was an heir to the Spanish throne, was sentenced to life in solitary confinement in Madrid's ancient prison called "The Place of the Skull." This was a very dreary, dirty, and fearsome place. In fact, everyone knew that once a person was put into The Place of the Skull, he would never come out alive.

When the Prince of Granada was sent to prison, the only book he was given to read was the Bible. Because that was the only thing he had to read, he read the Bible from cover to cover hundreds and hundreds of times. The Bible became his constant companion.

After being imprisoned for thirty-three years, the prince finally died. When the officials came in to clean out his cell, they found that he had made some notes using nails to mark on the soft walls of his cell. The notes were of this kind: "Psalm 118:8 is the middle verse of the Bible; Ezra 7:21 contains all the letters of the alphabet except the letter j; the ninth verse of the eighth chapter of Esther is the longest verse in the Bible; no word or name of more than six syllables can be found in the Bible."

Centuries later, a researcher wrote about the unfortunate prince in a popular journal called *Psychology Today*. He commented on how odd it was that a person like the prince could have spent thirty-three years of his life studying the most influential collection of books in the history of the world—the Bible—and only glean trivia. From what anybody knew, the prince had never made any type of spiritual commitment to Jesus Christ nor had his heart touched in any way by what he read. Rather, he simply became an expert on Bible trivia.

What a terribly sad story this is.

Like the prince in the story, you and I have been given the precious Bible. There are three main ways people can approach the Bible, two of them bad, and one of them good.

One way that some people approach the Bible is to take everything literally. These persons are sometimes called biblical literalists or fundamentalists. They are so committed to literal interpretation of the stories that they miss the message the stories are trying to teach. They ignore the cultural and temporal contexts of the books. They ignore or gloss over obvious inconsistencies within the Bible. They forget that the Bible is a collection of theology, a way to understand God and explain the workings of God using human stories and words, written by many hands over many centuries. Though the Bible contains history, it is not a history book. Though it has some biology, it is not a biology book. Though it has some architecture, it is not an architecture book.

A second way that the Bible can be abused is to trivialize it, to approach it as an academic exercise. Many people approach the Bible this way. They spend hours and hours memorizing things such as all the names of the books of the Bible, where everything is found in the Bible, and the like. This is useful insofar as it assists the person in genuine Bible study, but often such individuals love to show off their knowledge of chapters and verses for just about any topic that comes to mind. This approach to the Bible is not what Jesus called for. Furthermore, this approach is basically irrelevant in our times, for our computers already have this information for us.

The third approach, and the one Catholic Christians are called to follow, is to take the messages of the Bible stories, allow the messages to touch our hearts, and then put them into practice into everyday life. It is not sufficient to be able to cite the exact verse in Scripture, for example, where one can find the story of Jesus changing bread and wine into his Body and Blood. It is not enough to memorize a list of all the guests at the Last Supper. Rather, it is necessary for us

69

to see that these were precious gifts that Jesus gave us, gifts we are to treasure.

Further, as Catholic Christians, we are called not only to thank God for the gift of his son, but we are called to take and eat, take and drink of Holy Communion. And most importantly, we are then to become what we eat; we are to become like Christ.

That is exactly what we are doing in our parish for these two weekends. We are witnessing children and youth receiving First Communion. They are following Jesus' command. That is good. But then they will have to do the harder part: to become like Jesus more and more every day.

And that is the good news I have for you on this Third Sunday of Easter.

Story source: Les Christie, "The Prince of Granada," in Wayne Rice (Ed.), *Hot Illustrations for Youth Talks*, Grand Rapids, Michigan, Youth Specialties/Zondervan, 1993, pp. 165-166.

Chapter 18

4th Sunday of Easter 4 – B

Good Shepherds

<u>Scripture:</u>

- Acts 4: 8-12
- Psalm 118: 1 & 8-9, 21-23, 26 & 21 & 29
- 1 John 3: 1-2
- John 10: 11-18

Today, Catholic Christians celebrate the Fourth Sunday of Easter.

On this day, we hear Jesus telling his followers that he is the Good Shepherd, a shepherd so good that he is willing to lay down his life for his sheep. And because Christians are to be "like Christ," we too are called to be good shepherds. In the following story, though, we see that not everyone who is put in charge of sheep is a good shepherd.

Msgr. Joe Pelligrino tells the story of an American family that was delighted to learn that a distant relative in Scotland had left them all his property when he died. Included was a wool business that turned a little profit every year. Therefore, the family went to Scotland to determine whether or not they should continue the business.

They found a farm where a flock of four hundred sheep grazed on the hills. At first, they were very pleased, for everything seemed to be going well. But when they looked at the books, they found that five years earlier there had been a thousand sheep. When they asked the business manager about this, he told them that one year there was a flood, another year there were problems with thieves, and that it is hard to hire people willing to go into the hills to risk their lives and health for the sheep.

To understand why a good shepherd is hard to find, we have to understand the nature of sheep. Unlike many animals, domestic sheep are very vulnerable. They don't know how to protect themselves. Wolves and other animals of prey will kill them if a shepherd does not protect them. In other words, sheep need all the help they can get, and that's the job of a shepherd. A shepherd must be willing to give his or her whole self for the sheep.

In today's Gospel, Jesus calls himself the Good Shepherd. In this image, we are the sheep, the ones who need his guidance and protection. He is a "good" shepherd because he is willing to lay down his life to protect us. Specifically, Jesus says, "I am the good shepherd. A good shepherd lays down his life for the sheep. A hired man, who is not a shepherd and whose sheep are not his own, sees a wolf coming and leaves the sheep and runs away, and the wolf catches and scatters them. This is because he works for pay and has no concern for the sheep. I am the good shepherd, and I know mine and mine know me" (John 10: 11-14).

As Christians, we are called to follow Jesus. Thus, since Jesus is a good shepherd, then so must we be. We are called to be shepherds in various ways depending on our particular vocations.

Parents are the shepherds of the domestic church, the most basic level of church, which exists in the home. The parents' flock is their children. Parents are good shepherds when they protect their children from danger yet encourage them to explore their world and grow. They are good shepherds when they lead and teach Christian behavior not just by words, but also by example. Parents have unlimited opportunities to be good shepherds.

Teenagers are called to be good shepherds of their younger brothers and sisters. In many cultures, even kindergarteners are called to be shepherds of their baby brothers and sisters. In the mountain country of Uganda, for example, I often saw little girls of five or six years old carrying their baby brothers or sisters on their backs.

Little children can even be shepherds of their pets, protecting their dogs and cats from harm, seeing that they are well fed, and showing them love.

Pastors are shepherds of the next level of Church, the parish, a collection of domestic churches. Pastors are called to guide their flocks by preaching the Good News of Jesus Christ and living lives that model virtue. Pastors are also called to watch out for danger that could harm the flock, and get rid of the danger before it harms them.

Single people and married people without children also are shepherds of nieces and nephews, neighbor children, and those who work for them. In our parish, I am amazed at how much shepherding is done by singles and married persons without children. So many give their time and talent in serving the flock as catechists, counselors, missionaries, servants of the poor, and a host of other roles.

In short, all of us as Christians are called to be good shepherds practicing love, compassion, strength, perseverance, vigilance, and hard work on behalf of our respective flocks. In our parish this weekend, we joyfully witness children and youth receiving First Communion. We pray that they will become what they eat, that is, that they will become more and more like Jesus Christ. We pray that they will grow into good shepherds, always ready to give themselves to others for whom they are responsible.

As we continue our life journeys this week, perhaps we could ask ourselves some questions. Who makes up my flock? What kind of shepherd am I? Do I lead by example as well as by talk? Am I modeling Jesus Christ?

And that is the good news I have for you on this Fourth Sunday of Easter.

Story source: A sheep farm in Scotland story as told by Fr. (now Msgr.) Joe Pelligrino in his Internet homily of May 7, 2006.

Chapter 19

5th Sunday of Easter – B

Sounds of Mother's Day

Scripture:

- Acts 9: 26-31
- Psalm 22: 26b-27, 28 & 30, 31-32
- 1 John 3: 18-24
- John 15: 1-8

As we come together today to celebrate the Fifth Sunday of Easter, we hear from St. John how we are to love one another. That is the way we remain connected to Jesus, just as healthy branches are connected to a vine. And as John reminds us, we are called to show this love in deeds, not only in words.

Usually the loving deeds of we mere mortals are less than perfect. That is unimportant, for it is the love in our hearts that is more important than perfection in deeds. That is what we see in the following reflection by the late humorist Erma Bombeck, writing in honor of a Mother's Day past.

> On Mother's Day all over the country, grateful moms are pushed back into their pillows, the flower on their bird-of-paradise plant (which blooms every other year for fifteen minutes) is snipped and put in a shot glass, and a strange assortment of food comes out of a kitchen destined to take the sight from a good eye.
>
> A mixer whirls out of control, and then stops abruptly as a voice cries, "I'm telling." A dog barks and another voice says, "Get his paws out of there. Mom has to eat that!"
>
> Minutes pass and finally, "Dad! Where's the chili sauce?" Then, "Don't you dare bleed on Mom's breakfast!"
>
> The rest is a blur of banging doors, running water, rapid footsteps and a high-pitched, "You started the fire! You put it out!"
>
> The breakfast is fairly standard: a water tumbler of juice, five pieces of black bacon that snap in half when you breathe on them, a mound of eggs that would feed a Marine division, and four pieces of cold toast.
>
> The kids line up to watch you eat, and from time to time ask why you're not drinking your Kool-Aid or touching the cantaloupe with black olives on top, spelling M-O-M.

Later in the day, after you have decided it's easier to move to a new house than clean the kitchen, you return to your bed where, if you're wise, you'll reflect on this day. For the first time, your children have given instead of received. They have offered to you the sincerest form of flattery: trying to emulate what you do for them. And they have presented you with the greatest gift people can give: themselves.

There will be other Mother's Days and other gifts that will astound and amaze you. But not one of them will ever measure up to the sound of your children in the kitchen on Mother's Day whispering, "Don't you dare bleed on Mom's breakfast!"

What a beautiful Mother's Day story this is. In so many ways, it reflects all of us as we try to imitate God. Just as God shows his love for us by giving us an incredible array of gifts, we try to follow the Christian command to love others just as much as we love our selves.

And like the children in the story, we fall short of perfection. After all, we are human, not divine. But that is perfectly fine, for it is the love behind the gift that is important.

Each May, we celebrate Mother's Day in the United States, a day we honor those women who raise children. Mothers, like fathers, have unlimited opportunities to imitate God's love by putting their own love into deeds for their children. They show this love by nurturing and guiding, cooking and teaching, cheering and challenging, nursing and mentoring. From our mothers, we learn how to give as well as receive. As leaders of the domestic church, sometimes alone and sometimes with their husbands, mothers give love by teaching children to pray, telling stories of Jesus and God and the Bible, showing their children how to celebrate Christian rituals such as decorating a Christmas tree or coloring Easter eggs, and teaching basic values.

On behalf of the staff and faculty of our parish, I wish all mothers and mothers-to-be a very Happy Mother's Day, and a big "Thank you!" for all of the ways you put your love into action every day of your life.

And that is the good news I have for you on this Fifth Sunday of Easter.

Story source: Erma Bombeck, "The Sounds of Mother's Day," in William J. Bausch (Ed.), *A World of Stories for Preachers and Teachers,* Mystic, CT: Twenty-Third Publications 1998, #303, pp. 376-377.

Chapter 20

6th Sunday of Easter – B

Jesus as Friend

Scripture:

- Acts 10: 25-26, 34-35, 44-48
- Psalm 98: 1, 2-3ab, 3cd-4
- 1 John 4: 7-10
- John 15: 9-17

Today Catholic Christians celebrate the Sixth Sunday of Easter.

In today's Gospel reading from St. John, Jesus tells us that he is our friend if we do what he commands us to do.

Friendship, as we know, is a very precious gift. Without friends, our lives would be drab and lacking in joy. Sometimes, however, we take friendship for granted. We fail to realize just how precious our friendships are for our mental, spiritual, and physical well-being.

In the following story, we hear how two friends discovered how much they meant to each other and became able to live their lives more abundantly.

Lupe and Maria were long-time friends. They first met at a company they both worked for right after college. Eventually, they went their separate ways and didn't see each other very often. They did, however, keep in touch and loved getting together from time to time. When they did get together, it was as though they had never been apart.

One day, Lupe invited Maria to spend a few days vacationing at her beach house. Maria was thrilled to receive the invitation. She had been working very hard getting her stepfather settled into her home, and was grateful for the opportunity to spending some time with her best friend.

Ordinarily, when the two friends visited each other, their time together involved a whirlwind of activities such as visiting antique shops, art galleries, craft exhibits, restaurants, summer theaters, and the like. Maria found it a nice change of pace from her quiet country life.

This time, however, Maria was more in the mood for a quiet time, a time for rest and inactivity. Unfortunately, as soon as Maria got to Lupe's beach house, Lupe began taking Maria to all sorts of places. Maria put up with all this hectic activity for a day or two, but then one evening she exploded. She said, "Can't you ever stay still? Don't you see I'm tired?"

Poor Lupe was devastated. Then Maria, sorry she had hurt Lupe's feelings, said, "I need time with you, time to enjoy your friendship."

Lupe replied, "That's what I want also. I thought, though, that you would find quiet time with me very dull."

Maria replied, "You are anything but dull!"

Once the women learned that they both wanted quiet time together sharing their friendships, they had a wonderful time. They enjoyed the rest of their vacation talking, walking on the beach, cooking their own meals, and just basking in their friendship. When their vacation was over, they were not tired out from a whirlwind of activities. Rather, each returned to her daily life refreshed and filled with renewed zest.

For the past few weeks in our Sunday readings, Jesus has been trying to tell the disciples who he is. Last week, for example, we heard Jesus likening himself to a vine, with us being the branches. The week before that, Jesus likened himself to a good shepherd who is willing to lay down his life for us, his sheep. Today, however, Jesus is telling us that he is our friend. Not only are we his friends, but also that it was he who chose us to be his friends. Imagine that! What a radical concept that is, that God the Son would pick us out of all the people on Earth to be his friends.

Unfortunately, however, we often lose sight of this image of Jesus. For example, how many times have you heard of Catholic parishes with lofty names like Christ the King, Good Shepherd, or Prince of Peace? But have you ever heard of a Catholic parish named "Jesus the Friend" or "Christ the Friend?" I certainly have never heard of such a parish name. Why do you suppose that is?

Perhaps it is that many of us think of Jesus as too far removed from us to actually be our friend. We might think that we are so insignificant compared to him, that Jesus could never actually be our friend. Or we might think of ourselves as too unworthy to be a friend of God the Son.

But Jesus explicitly said that we are his friends, and that he chose us. With that realization, we ask ourselves what makes a good friend.

A friend is someone who is always there for us. A friend rejoices in our good times and feels sad when we are sad. A friend is someone with whom we can simply spend quiet time without talking. A friend is someone who laughs with us when we find the world funny. A friend challenges us, urging us to new and greater heights. A friend is someone gives us a kick in the pants when we are too down on ourselves.

I'm sure you can list many more qualities of a good friend.

As we continue our life journeys this week, it would be good to reflect on the fact that Jesus has told us that we are his friends. The real question is, "How do I reciprocate this friendship?" How do I treat Jesus as a friend? How do I spend time with him? What do I share with him? What makes him smile? What makes him sad? How do I recognize that he is walking beside me every moment of every day?

And that is the good news I have for you on this Sixth Sunday of Easter.

Story source: Anonymous, "The Visit," in William J. Bausch (Ed.), *A World of Stories for Preachers & Teachers*, Mystic, CT: Twenty-Third Publications, 1998, #83, pp. 231-232.

Chapter 21

Ascension – B

Dolley Pond

<u>Scripture:</u>

- Acts 1: 1-11
- Psalm 47: 2-3, 6-7, 8-9
- Ephesians 4: 1-13
- Mark 16: 15-20

Today, most Catholic Christians in the United States celebrate the Feast of the Ascension of the Lord. This feast commemorates Jesus' Ascension into heaven after he had spent some time with his disciples following his resurrection from the dead.

After giving his disciples the command to "go into the whole world and proclaim the gospel to every creature," Jesus said a most amazing thing about those who would believe the good news the disciples preached. He said of the new-found believers: "These signs will accompany those who believe: in my name they will drive out demons, they will speak new languages. They will pick up serpents with their hands, and if they drink any deadly thing, it will not harm them. They will lay hands on the sick, and they will recover" (Mark 16: 17-18).

For the majority of Christians, this passage is designed to teach a moral: good things will happen if you believe in Jesus. However, there have been some who have taken this literally to prove to others that God is on their side. Take the fascinating case of George Went Hensley, also known as "Little George."

Hensley was a former bootlegger who became ordained a preacher in the Church of God of Prophecy in 1909. This was a new denomination in the Holiness and Pentecostal traditions. Hensley quickly made a name for himself by bringing live rattlesnakes and other deadly snakes to his services. He wanted to show that if people are filled with the Holy Spirit, they could handle deadly snakes. He also encouraged his followers to drink what many called "Holy Ghost cocktails" containing strychnine.

The Church of God of Prophecy tolerated George Hensley for some years, but then they realized they had made a mistake in ordaining him. So, in 1928, the denomination expelled him. Not to be defeated, Hensley and some friends founded a new church called the Dolley Pond Church of God with Signs Following in Pine Mountain, Tennessee. From this church grew a new denomination noted for lively music, dancing with snakes, shouting, speaking in tongues, being "slain by the Spirit," and fundamentalist preaching.

Sociologists know that members of this denomination – The Church of God with Signs Following - usually have very little formal education and are either unemployed or in very low-paying jobs. Lacking power in the real world, their strength is in church services where they can demonstrate the power of God. Thus, handling snakes and drinking poisons helps members show that God indeed loves them in a very special way. Thus, even though they are marginal in the world of Christianity, they feel that the fact they can handle deadly things is proof that they have a special relationship with God.

These followers believe that if a person is bitten by a deadly snake during a religious ceremony, it could mean one of five things: (1) the person has sin in his or her life; (2) he or she is not anointed by the Holy Spirit; (3) he or she lacks faith to handle serpents; (4) that God is testing the person's faith; or (5) God has allowed the bite so he can demonstrate his healing power.

Now I think it is safe to say that most Americans frown on snake-handling and poison-drinking religious ceremonies. But what they might fail to realize is that they themselves do things to convince themselves or others that God loves them more than others. It is likely that this has been going on in all religions since the dawn of time.

Some people, for example, flaunt their spirituality. Like the Pharisees of Jesus' time, these folks like to parade around acting "holier-than-thou." They see themselves as a "cut above" others, and they tend to look down on others for not being as close to God as they are. Perhaps you felt that way when hearing about the Dolley Pond Church of God with Signs Following. Often such people are hypercritical and judgmental of others, quick to find the specks in others' eyes while ignoring the planks in their own.

Others believe that financial success is "proof" that God loves them. They believe that because they don't suffer joblessness or other calamities that others experience, that it means God favors them above others. They may even demean the faith of poor people.

Still others believe that being in a particular religion or denomination means that God loves them better than others. Catholics may feel God loves them better than Baptists or Hindus. Jews may think God loves them better than gentiles. Believers in God may think God loves them better than atheists. The list goes on and on and on.

Well, I've got news for you. God loves you—every single human being. God loves you if you are rich or poor, black or white or red or yellow or brown. God loves you if you're young or old, tall or short, gay or straight, progressive or conservative, American or Mexican, born or unborn, healthy or sick, or whatever. God loves everyone.

So, guess what? You don't have to try to "prove" God loves you. You can simply bask in the realization that God loves you and God loves all others. With that knowledge, act accordingly.

And that is the good news I have for you on this Ascension Sunday.

Story source: Dennis Covington, *Salvation on Sand Mountain: Snake Handling & Redemption in Southern Appalachia*, Philadelphia, PA: Da Capo Press, 2009.

Chapter 22

Pentecost – B

Keeper of the Springs

<u>Scripture:</u>

- Acts 2: 1-11
- Psalm 104: 1ab & 24ac, 29bc-30, 31 & 34
- Galatians 5: 16-25
- John 15: 26-27; 16: 12-15

Today Catholic Christians celebrate the Feast of Pentecost, the birthday of the Catholic Church in particular and Christianity in general.

Pentecost celebrates the day the Holy Spirit came down on the early disciples and enriched them with various gifts. Though each person has a different set of gifts, all gifts are to be used for the benefit of all. Sometimes, though, we minimize our gifts. We may think they are not important enough to benefit the Church. We may think that because we exercise the gifts "behind the scenes," they are not worthy. As we see in the following story, however, every gift is precious, and every gift can serve the Lord.

Once there was an old man who lived high above an Austrian village in the Alps. The Village Council had hired him many years before to clear away sticks and leaves and other debris from the pools of water in the mountain crevices that fed the beautiful stream that flowed through their village. And the old man did his job with great faithfulness. Each day, he patrolled the hills and removed leaves and branches, and he wiped away the silt that could choke and contaminate the fresh flow of water. Because of their beautiful stream, the mountain village became a popular tourist attraction. People loved to see the graceful swans floating in the crystal stream. Picnickers ate along the banks of the stream, and patrons eating in local cafes could watch the beautiful stream from the windows.

Many years passed, and the old man quietly and faithfully kept the stream clear from his home high above the village. One evening, the Village Council met for its semiannual meeting. When they reviewed the budget, they noticed that for many years they had been paying a small sum of money to someone called the "keeper of the spring." The Treasurer of the Village, always concerned about money, asked who this "keeper of the spring" was. He wanted to know why this expense had been incurred year after year. The treasurer found that although the "keeper" was an actual person high up in the mountains, no one on the Village Council had ever seen this "keeper of the spring." Thinking that this person was simply taking money each year and actually doing nothing, the treasurer recommended eliminating this expense. Everyone on the Village Council agreed, so the old man was dismissed.

For several weeks, nothing changed. The village went about its business as usual. But when autumn came, the leaves and small branches began to fall from the trees, falling into the pools that fed the stream and hindering the rushing flow of crystal clear water. One afternoon, someone in the village remarked that the beautiful stream had a strange yellow-brown tint. A couple of days later, the water's color became even darker. Within another week or two, a slimy film developed on sections of the water near the banks, and the people began to notice a foul odor. The swans left the village, and so did the tourists. Soon the economy of the village declined. Worse yet, many of the villagers began to get sick from drinking the water.

The Village Council called an emergency meeting. After discussing the problem, they realized that they had made a big mistake in firing the "keeper of the spring." Therefore, they hired back the old man. Within a few weeks, the beautiful stream came back to life. The swans and visitors returned, and the little village in the Alps once again came alive.

I think that most people use their gifts much like the "keeper of the springs," doing necessary and useful things in relative obscurity. How many tasks, for example, does a parent perform each day that no one in this world will ever know? Rather, parents do their ministry faithfully "behind the scenes."

In parish life, it's usually the priest who gets all the glory. He is the one that everyone sees, and he is the one who gets the compliments. Here in our parish, for example, many people compliment me on the new landscaping we have in front of and beside the church, the new railing we have that assists the elderly get into church, the new pre-school playground, our new dental clinic, our newly revised wedding banquet facility called *The Upper Room 1871,* and many other things.

But I know that although I gave the go-ahead for these things, I am not the one who planned and constructed and planted and paid for these things. It was a host of people doing ministries behind the scenes that made all these things happen. For each person to do his or her part is what the Pentecost experience is all about. But it's also about recognizing and appreciating the work of others in building and sustaining our community.

As we go about our life journey this weekend, let's take some time to think of all the ways we use our gifts and exercise our various ministries. How do our ministries help build up the Kingdom of God here on Earth? Let's also think about the contributions of so many others, and give credit and appreciation where it's due.

And that is the good news I have for you on this Pentecost Sunday.

Story source: Anonymous. "Keeper of the Springs," in Brian Cavanaugh (Ed.), *More Sower's Seeds: Second Planting*, Mystic, CT: Twenty-Third Publications, 1992, #75, pp. 73-74.

Part Three

෴

ORDINARY TIME

Chapter 23

Holy Trinity B

Fr. Vincent Capodanno

Scripture:

- Deuteronomy 4: 32-34, 39-40
- Psalm 33: 4-5, 6 & 9, 18-19, 20 & 22
- Romans 8: 14-17
- Matthew 28: 16-20

Today, Catholic Christians celebrate the Feast of the Most Holy Trinity.

On this day, we hear Jesus telling his disciples: "All power in heaven and on earth has been given to me. Go, therefore, and make disciples of all nations, baptizing them in the name of the Father, and of the Son, and of the Holy Spirit, teaching them to observe all that I have commanded you. And behold, I am with you always, until the end of the age" (Matthew 28: 18-20).

Although Jesus was speaking directly to his disciples, his words were also directed to us. After all, when we were baptized, we became anointed ministers of the Church. We too are disciples of Jesus Christ.

Most Christians proclaim the good news of Jesus by living out their vocations in their homes and workplaces in ways that are beneficial to others.

But there are always certain people the Lord calls to serve him in extraordinary ways. One such person was Vincent Robert Capodanno.

Vincent was born in February of 1929 in Staten Island, New York. After high school, he attended Fordham University for a year before entering Maryknoll to study to become a missionary priest.

He was ordained in June of 1957 and was sent to the mountains of Taiwan where he served in a parish and later a school. After serving in Taiwan for seven years, he was assigned to a Maryknoll school in Hong Kong.

In 1965, Fr. Vincent received permission to serve as a military chaplain, and in December, he was commissioned as a Lieutenant in the Navy Chaplain Corps. He was assigned to the First Marine Division in Vietnam in April 1966.

He had a fierce loyalty to the men he called "my Marines," and he earned the nickname, "The Grunt Padre."

On September 4, 1967, Fr. Vincent went with his men to serve a small unit of American Marines who were under heavy fire from approximately 2,500 North Vietnamese soldiers. Fr. Vincent went among the wounded and dying, anointing those he could. Though he was wounded in the face and his hand was nearly severed from his arm, he insisted the medical corpsmen serve the fighting men, not him. As he went to help one Navy medic, he was killed by enemy machine gun fire. He was only thirty-eight years old.

In December of 1968, the Secretary of the Navy notified Fr. Vincent's family that he was being given the Medal of Honor. The citation reads:

> For conspicuous gallantry and intrepidity at the risk of his life above and beyond the call of duty as Chaplain of the 3rd Battalion, in connection with operations against enemy forces. In response to reports that the 2nd Platoon of M Company was in danger of being overrun by a massed enemy assaulting force, Lt. Capodanno left the relative safety of the company command post and ran through an open area raked with fire, directly to the beleaguered platoon. Disregarding the intense enemy small-arms, automatic-weapons, and mortar fire, he moved about the battlefield administering last rites to the dying and giving medical aid to the wounded. When an exploding mortar round inflicted painful multiple wounds to his arms and legs, and severed a portion of his right hand, he steadfastly refused all medical aid. Instead, he directed the corpsmen to help their wounded comrades and, with calm vigor, continued to move about the battlefield as he provided encouragement by voice and example to the valiant Marines. Upon encountering a wounded corpsman in the direct line of fire...he was struck down by a burst of machine gun fire. By his heroic conduct on the battlefield, and his inspiring example, Lt. Capodanno upheld the finest traditions of the U.S. Naval Service. He gallantly gave his life in the cause of freedom.

The American government has honored Fr. Capodanno by having a ship named after him as well as chapels in Iraq, Vietnam, Italy, Japan, Taiwan, and several American states. The biggest honor, though, was being named "Servant of God" on May 19, 2006. That means that Fr. Capodanno is now on the way to becoming a Saint of the Catholic

Church. You can read more about this Maryknoll missionary priest in the book by Fr. Daniel Mode called *The Grunt Padre*.

Most of us will never have the honor of giving our lives like Fr. Capodanno in an inspirational "blaze of glory," but all of us are called to witness to Jesus Christ by living our lives in such a way that we are lights to the world.

And that is the good news I have for you on this Feast of the Most Holy Trinity.

Story source: Fr. Daniel L. Mode, *The Grunt Padre*, Oak Lawn, IL: CMJ Marian Publishers, 2000.

Chapter 24

Most Holy Body & Blood of Christ B

Passover and Eucharist

Scripture:

- Exodus 24: 3-8
- Psalm 116: 12-13, 15 & 16bc, 17-18
- Hebrews 9: 11-15
- Mark 14: 12-16, 22-26

Today we celebrate the Feast of the Most Holy Body and Blood of Christ, sometimes called *Corpus Christi*.

Because Catholic Christianity is often called the "Flower of Judaism," and because the first time that Eucharist was celebrated was at the Passover celebration, it is good for Catholic Christians to understand Passover to understand Mass, that is, the Eucharist.

Passover is an eight-day observance commemorating the exodus of the Israelites from slavery in Egypt, centuries before Christ. The English word "Passover," *Pesach* in Hebrew, stems from God's instruction to the Israelites to mark their homes so that while punishing the Egyptians he would "pass over" the Israelite families. At Passover time, families gather to celebrate this feast with a special meal called a *Seder*. The primary Jewish place of worship is the home, specifically around the kitchen table.

To prepare for a *Seder*, which is usually held on the first and sometimes second night of Passover, the house is cleaned very thoroughly, and all foods that contain yeast, such as bread and rolls, are discarded. The regular dishes and silverware are put away, and special Passover dishes and silverware are taken out and cleaned.

Only foods that are called "Kosher for Passover" are allowed for the *Seder*. A special *Seder* plate is put in the center of the table with five special foods commemorating the journey of the Jews from bondage: *Haroseth* (a special mixture of chopped walnuts, apples, raisins, and other things); parsley; roasted egg; a shank bone; and bitter herbs, often symbolized by horseradish. At the meal, four glasses of wine are poured to represent the four stages of deliverance from Egypt.

A major part of the *Seder* is the telling of the story of God's salvation of the Israelites from their Egyptian slavery. In telling the stories, the children are engaged in the *Seder* by a series of questions focusing around the biggest question of all, "Why is this night different from every other night?"

The children learn about the ten plagues that God sent upon Egypt: blood, frogs, vermin, flies, cattle disease, boils, hail, locusts, darkness, and the slaying of the firstborn of both humans and beasts. The children learn that Passover means a "passing over" or "protection." They learn that God told the Hebrews to mark their dwellings with blood of the Paschal lamb so that God could "pass over" their homes and not kill the firstborn in their houses. The children learn about the symbolism of each of the special foods on the Passover plate. They learn about why ordinary bread has disappeared from the table and now only unleavened bread, or *matzo*, is present.

In summary, the Passover *Seder* is the central feature of Passover. This is what Jesus was celebrating when he instituted the Eucharist or Mass.

Unfortunately, through the ages the clergy took the Eucharist away from the average, everyday Catholic Christian and suppressed the historical connection with the chosen people's salvation from slavery. The Eucharist began to be celebrated not in the language of the people, as the first Eucharist was celebrated, but rather in a language that few understood. Instead of celebrating the Eucharist as a Passover celebration, which is traditionally interactive in nature, it began to be the private domain of the priest. The Catholic Christians became mere observers.

Because they were so removed from the celebration of Eucharist or Mass, the people began to see the consecrated Host and Precious Blood as something separate from Eucharist. Thus, they began to invent certain pious practices detached from the Eucharistic celebration such as Forty Hours devotion, Benediction, and the like. This behavior may be compared to a Jewish person who eats some fancy lamb chops in a restaurant and then claims to have celebrated Passover.

The feast we celebrate today, the Body and Blood of Christ, is one that grew out of the Middle Ages when the Body and Blood of Christ were detached from the Eucharist itself. The message we have today, in light of the teaching of the Second Vatican Council, is that while we adore Christ in the sacred Host and Precious Blood, we must never forget that we are to celebrate the Eucharist, or Mass, in community. The Eucharist is about community and about stories from the Old and New Testaments. It is about worshiping God the Father. It is about the priest asking God the Father to send God the Holy Spirit to change bread and wine into the Body and Blood of Christ. It is about praying for our Church and the salvation of all humanity.

So today as we continue our life journeys, let us remember that the consecrated elements are just part of Eucharist, the Passover heritage that Christianity, the "Flower of Judaism," has treasured for more than two thousand years. With this insight, perhaps it would be a good idea to learn more about Passover as well as Eucharist or Mass. After all, as we learn from the Second Vatican Council, the Eucharist or Mass is the "source and summit" of Catholic Christian spirituality. If this is the case, it is a very good idea to learn all we can about the Eucharistic celebration.

And that is the good news I have for you on this Feast of the Most Holy Body and Blood of Christ.

Chapter 25

2nd Sunday in Ordinary Time – B

Brother Bill

Scripture:

- 1 Samuel 3: 3b-10, 19
- Psalm 40: 2 & 4ab, 7-8a, 8b-9, 10
- 1 Corinthians 6: 13c-15a, 17-20
- John 1: 35-42

Today Catholic Christians celebrate the Second Sunday in Ordinary Time.

In today's Old Testament reading, we hear God calling Samuel (1 Samuel 3: 3b-10, 19), and in the Gospel, we hear how Jesus called Simon Peter and Peter's brother Andrew to follow him (John 1: 35-42). Though their calls were different, the men followed the Lord to the best of their abilities.

Each of us has a call - something God wants us to do with our lives. Many of us receive different callings depending on the stage of life we are in. That is what happened to Bill Tome, a native of Chicago.

Bill was raised in a fine Catholic home and had an excellent education at Loyola Academy and the University of Notre Dame, graduating in 1959. After receiving a master's degree in guidance and counseling, Bill worked for sixteen years for Catholic Charities in Chicago. He led a very ordinary layman's life. While working on his doctorate, which he never completed, he made many trips to Europe, including Lourdes, France. There he made friends with the Virgin Mary.

In 1978, Bill quit his job with Catholic Charities and tried to be an artist, but found he did not have the patience for that. In 1980, he went looking for another career.

One day, he stopped into a small Ukrainian Catholic church to think and pray. Suddenly, the colors in the church all turned black, while what was white remained white. Everything was fuzzy except the face of Jesus near the altar. Christ spoke to Bill saying: "Love. You are forbidden to do anything other than that." Bill tried to get more information, but the Lord simply said, "I'll lead. You follow."

Bill gradually gave away all his possessions and began to volunteer at St. Malachy's church in a run-down area of Chicago. African-Americans now populated this parish, which formerly had been filled with Irish and Italian families. The pastor recommended that Bill wear some kind of habit to identify himself as part of the Church and to call himself "Brother Bill." Bill did just that, creating a habit out of old blue jeans.

Bill began to work with gangs. He loved the youth he met and treated them with unconditional love. He tried to make the young men feel good about themselves, to stop being violent, to make something of their lives. He was so successful in working with poor youth that Cardinal Bernadin eventually put him on the payroll of the Archdiocese of Chicago.

I imagine that when many of you hear the story of Brother Bill, you are saying, "Well, sure. Jesus spoke directly to him. If Christ spoke directly to me, it would make my vocational journey much easier."

The truth of the matter is, though, that Jesus *has* spoken to us though the Scriptures. When he called his disciples to follow him, he was speaking to the generations. Remember that at our baptism we became his disciples, his followers. Therefore, the call of "follow me" is just as relevant to you and me as it was to Peter, James, John, and the other early leaders of the Church.

But how exactly do we know what God is calling us to do specifically?

First, God calls all of us to fulfill the triple love command in our everyday lives, that is, to love God, love others, as we love ourselves.

Second, we learn of God's plan for our lives by eliminating those things we know would not fulfill us. For example, I have always known I would rather work indoors than outdoors. That leaves out many occupations. I have also always known that I didn't want to work in sports or manufacturing or business.

Third, we pay attention to the desires God has planted in our hearts. I have always wanted to be a priest, a writer, a health care professional, a professor, and a scientist. With God's help, I have been able to become a priest, an R.N., a writer, a university professor, and a sociologist. I have also always wanted to be a missionary in a foreign land, but that seems to be an aspect of my life that will not be fulfilled until after I retire from active parish ministry when I'm seventy-five years old.

Fourth, we ask ourselves if we have the qualifications to become what we think God is calling us to become. For example St. Therese, the Little Flower, wanted to be a priest and a foreign missionary. However, she did not have the physical strength to be a missionary, and she was not of the correct gender to become a Catholic priest. Thus, she was able to rule out those choices from her list of how to follow the Lord.

Finally, we receive messages from God via the world around us, from our family, friends, acquaintances, and coworkers. We get clues from movies and radio programs and television and newspapers. We get clues from reading autobiographies, biographies such as lives of the saints, and history books. God continuously sends us messages through the world around us.

As we continue our life journeys this week, it would be good to reflect on how God is calling you to follow him.

And that is the good news I have for you on this Second Sunday in Ordinary Time.

Story source: Tim Unsworth, "Brother Bill: Unconditional Love," in Tim Unsworth (Ed.), *Here Comes Everybody!: Stories of Church*, New York: Catholic Publishing Company, 1993, pp. 120-131.

Chapter 26

3rd Sunday in Ordinary Time – B

A South African Christian

Scripture:

- Jonah 3: 1-5, 10
- Psalm 25: 4-5ab, 6 & 7bc, 8-9
- 1 Corinthians 7: 29-31
- Mark 1: 14-20

Today Catholic Christians celebrate the Third Sunday in Ordinary Time.

In today's Gospel reading, we hear Jesus call two sets of brothers – Simon and Andrew, and James and John – to drop what they were doing and follow him. When Jesus called the men, Simon and Andrew were fishing, and James and John were mending their nets on the shore of the lake. Though all four men were busy, they immediately put down what they were doing and followed Jesus (Mark 1: 16-20).

Sometimes when we hear such stories, we think that such a calling does not apply to us. We might say, "Well, Jesus has never come to me as he did to those men." Or we might say, "Well, those men were chosen to be Apostles. I'm not an apostle."

But such stories, called "vocation stories," do apply to us. True, even though we were not called to be one of the Twelve Apostles, and even though Jesus has not appeared to us in bodily form just as he did to those men, he is still calling us to follow him, to be his disciples.

At our Baptism, the Holy Spirit entered into us. We became disciples of Jesus Christ, anointed ministers of his Church. This sacrament is permanent.

Our call to discipleship is not specific in terms of an occupation. On the contrary, every person who is baptized is called to serve out his or her ministry in everyday life. We are to be lights to the world, always ready to serve as beacons of love to all those around us.

Sometimes, though, we forget our incredibly noble calling. Sometimes we get so lost in our ordinariness that we forget the special nature of our Christianity. The man in the following story was one person who did not forget.

The story takes place in South Africa in the 1960s. At that time, life was incredibly difficult for black Africans, who were denied equality by law. One day, two businessmen, Mr. Rumbold and Mr. Samuel, stopped in a restaurant for lunch. When they sat down at their table, they took off their suit jackets and hung them over their chairs. Later that day, as Mr. Rumbold went to get his money and coupons to pay for some gasoline on the road, he discovered that his wallet was missing.

Three days later, as the two businessmen were driving back to Johannesburg, a middle-aged black African man, dressed in shorts, waved them down. "Are you going to Johannesburg?" he asked. When the businessmen told the black man they were indeed going there, the black man said, "Would you please try to find a Mr. Rumbold there and give him this wallet? I found it three days ago in the street."

Mr. Rumbold was incredulous. Everything, including the cash and gasoline coupons, was intact. The poor, humble man refused a reward saying, "No, sir. I do not need to be rewarded for not stealing. I am a Christian."

If you are like me, you might be asking yourself, "Would I have done the same thing?" Would I actually have left the wallet intact after three days? Or would I have spent the money after a day or two of not finding the owner?

The black African man had a profound realization of his Christian identify. For him, being Christian was an "always" thing. He was not just a Christian when he went to Church services. He was a Christian all the time in all aspects of his life.

Like the man who found the wallet, all of us are called by the Lord to be his disciples.

We are called to be his disciples at home with our families. We are called to nurture our children and show love and compassion to other family members.

We are called to be disciples of Jesus in our workplace, always doing a good day's work for a day's wage. We are disciples when we work just as hard when the boss is out of town as when the boss in the building.

We are called to be disciples at leisure. For example, in a restaurant we show our Christian identity when we bow our heads and say a prayer before our meal. Catholic Christians should not be ashamed to make the sign of the cross before and after their prayer.

We are called to be disciples in everyday life. As we approach a stranded motorist on the side of the road, for example, we show our discipleship by at least using our cell phone to call for help if the person needs such assistance.

We show our discipleship by our generosity towards those in need. Such generosity might be shown by giving alms to the poor, funds to support missionaries in poor lands, visiting the sick, visiting those in prison, donating clothes or food to social outreach ministries, or other acts of kindness.

All of these are acts of discipleship. All make us "a light to the world."

As we continue our life journeys this week, let's take some time to reflect on our own lives. Are we 24-hour-a-day Christians? Or do we allow our Christianity to come and go depending on how we feel at any given moment?

And that is the good news I have for you on this Third Sunday in Ordinary Time.

Story source: "A Christian!" from *The Des Moines Register* (December 5, 1968) in G.Curtin Jones & Paul H. Jones (Eds.), *500 Illustrations: Stories from Life for Preaching & Teaching,* Edited by G. Curtin Jones & Paul H. Jones, Nashville: Abington Press, 1998, p. 69.

Chapter 27

4th Sunday in Ordinary Time – B

Helping the Third Level of Church

Scripture:

- Deuteronomy 18: 15-20
- Psalm 95: 1-2, 6-7c, 7d-9
- 1 Corinthians 7: 32-35
- Mark 1: 21-28

The first person that we know to have used the term "The Catholic Church" to refer to all of the various communities of early Christianity was St. Ignatius of Antioch, an Apostolic Father who was third Bishop of Antioch.

Through the ages, the Church has come to see itself as a living, dynamic organism. The Church on Earth is organized on four different levels.

The first level of Church is composed of individuals and families. It is on this level that parents, as priests of the domestic church, lead their flock. We all become priests at our baptism in what we call the "priesthood of all believers." This type of priest, although different in both kind and nature from the ordained priest, is very important. The priests of the domestic church teach their flock how to pray, instill basic values, teach them about the Faith, help them read the Bible, tell them stories about God, Jesus, saints and heroes, and lead them in celebrating Christian rituals. We work to nurture the domestic Church every day.

The second level of Church is called "the parish." Parishes are headed by an ordained priest and are a collection of individuals and domestic churches, that is, families, who come together to worship the Lord in community. Parishes serve the local community with many ministries.

The third level of Church is called "the diocese" and that is the level on which today's homily focuses. Sometimes the diocese is called the "Local Church." Our diocese is called the Diocese of Raleigh, and is headed by a bishop who is responsible for shepherding all the Catholic Christians in this diocese. Dioceses are usually geographical areas. Our diocese is composed of the 54 eastern counties of North Carolina. Catholic Christians are called to help support the ministries of the diocese once a year in what is called the Bishop's Annual Appeal. So, while we support the domestic church every day, and the parish once a week, we support the diocese once a year.

The fourth level is, of course, the universal Church.

This Bishop's Annual Appeal is a six-month period going from February to July. The bishop uses funds raised in this campaign to fund diocese-wide church efforts such as Campus ministries, Seminarian education, Catechist formation, Catholic school development, Hispanic ministries, Deacon formation, Catholic Charities, African American ministries, the North Carolina Home Mission Society, and many other ministries. Without our help, the bishop could not serve us as effectively as he does.

Each year, the Bishop's Annual Appeal has a particular financial goal. Each parish, in turn, is given a goal based on how much offertory it raised during the past year. For example, if our parish offertory was 2% of all the offertory collections of all the parishes in the diocese, then our BAA goal this year would be 2% of the total BAA goal. Our parish goal is over $122,000 for this year. That is a great increase over last year's goal of $88,000 because our parish had one of the greatest increases in offertory of any parish in the diocese. It's a challenge, but in fact our generous parishioners pledged more money last year than this year's goal. So we should be in good shape if we all do our part again.

Like last year, I'm asking you to consider a minimum pledge of $11.50 per week for six months. (That is the cost of one large pizza per week.) In other words, it would be about $50 per month or $300 for the whole campaign. Many of you, of course, can do much more. I always do double or triple what I ask of you. In this case, I'll do triple and add some on top of that to make it more than last year's contribution.

Before you make your pledge, ask yourself if you're going to go to bed hungry tonight. Will you be warm enough? Will you even have a bed and a house?

In the time it has taken to give this homily, 720 children in this world have died from hunger alone. This day more than 25,000 people in the world will die of hunger and poverty. And more than 820,000,000 will be hungry at bedtime.

Though Americans are in tough economic times, our troubles cannot begin to compare with those who live in the world of constant needs, not wants. Today more than ever, God is calling those of us who have so much to be more generous than ever.

Can I afford a measly $11.50 per week to support my diocese? Can I afford not to?!

And that is the good news I have for you on this Fourth Sunday in Ordinary Time.

Chapter 28

5th Sunday in Ordinary Time – B

The Caliph's Son

Scripture:

- Job 7: 1-4, 6-7
- Psalm 147: 1-2, 3-4, 5-6
- 1 Corinthians 9: 16-19, 22-23
- Mark 1: 29-39

Today Catholic Christians celebrate the Fifth Sunday in Ordinary Time.

In today's reading from St. Paul's first letter to the Corinthians, we learn a very important point about spreading the good news of Jesus Christ. To be credible to the people we are trying to reach, we need to understand their life circumstances as best we can. We need to feel their pain, experience their concerns, and learn their hopes and dreams. Only then can we be effective missionaries. Specifically, Paul says, "Although I am free in regard to all, I have made myself a slave to all so as to win over as many as possible. To the weak I became weak, to win over the weak. I have become all things to all, to save at least some. All this I do for the sake of the gospel, so that I too may have a share in it" (1 Corinthians 9: 19, 22-23).

In the following story, we hear about how a young prince grasped the wisdom that St. Paul advocated for Christians.

There was once a young prince by the name of Harun al-Rashid. He lived between the eighth and ninth Centuries in Baghdad in the country now known as Iraq.

One day, while riding his horse through the city, he noticed that many of the people seemed to be very unhappy about something. When he returned to the palace, he asked his father, the Caliph (which is like a king), why the people were unhappy. The caliph told his son not to worry about it. He told his son to play and ignore people's concerns.

The little prince, though, was a very curious boy. He kept asking people in the palace why people in the kingdom were so unhappy, but nobody had any idea.

Fortunately, the little prince was wise as well as curious. Therefore, one night, when everybody in the palace was asleep, the little prince dressed himself in rags and crept out of the castle into the streets of Baghdad. There he pretended to be a poor traveler, and he went from house to house to meet the people. When he would get to a house, he would ask for something to drink or for a bite of food or just to warm himself up by the fire. Most of the people welcomed him into their homes and shared what they could with him. Nobody ever guessed that this stranger was actually a prince.

In every home the prince entered, he listened carefully to what the people were saying. On this night, he learned so much about the people and their problems that he began to sneak out every night to learn more and more about the regular people.

He heard about how people could not find job, about how they often didn't have enough money to feed their families, and about how high their taxes were. He also heard complaining about his father, the caliph, and how he took their taxes and spent it on the army instead of on the basic needs of the people. The prince heard the people complaining about all the money the caliph spent on fancy clothes for the royal family and how the royal family lived in luxury.

After many years, his father died and the prince became the caliph of Baghdad. He immediately lowered the people's taxes. He spent much less money on himself and his family. He made sure everyone in the land had enough to eat and had a job. Often he would disguise himself as a beggar and go back into the streets of Baghdad to learn first-hand how things were going for his subjects.

Now when he rode through the streets, he only saw smiles. When he huddled in disguise with them beside their fireplaces, he heard the people talk about how their caliph was the wisest ruler they had ever had.

The people loved him so much that someone even wrote a book about him called *The Book of One Thousand and One Nights.*

The secret of Harun al-Rashid's success as a ruler was that he was willing to learn about his people from their perspective. He did not live a life so detached from his subjects that he was oblivious to their fears and hopes and dreams and struggles. On the contrary, he walked among them and learned as much as he could.

This is exactly what St. Paul was talking about in his First Letter to the Corinthians that we encounter today. We cannot be effective missionaries of our Faith—and every Catholic Christian is called to be a missionary—if we do not know the people to whom we are carrying Jesus' message of love. We need to be part of the people, not detached from them.

That is one of the reasons priests are called to be the servants of the people, to put themselves last. That is why Jesus washed the feet of his apostles, to show them that be the leader, one must be the servant of all, always willing to put others' needs ahead of one's own.

Priests of the domestic church—parents—know this well. Their children's welfare always comes first. Parents willing forgo buying themselves a new winter coat if their children need dental work or some other thing.

As we continue our life journeys this week, let's take some time to reflect on our own lives. How do I put the needs of others ahead of my own? How do I model Jesus in serving others? How do I sometimes fail by putting myself ahead of those I am called to serve?

And that is the good news I have for you on this Fifth Sunday in Ordinary Time.

Story source: Story of the Caliph's Son, in Thomas W. Goodhue's *Sharing the Good News with Children: Stories for the Common Lectionar0,*. Cincinnati, Ohio: St. Anthony Messenger Press, 1992, pp. 134-135.

Chapter 29

6th Sunday in Ordinary Time – B

St. Damien of Molokai

Scripture:

- Leviticus 13: 1-2, 44-46
- Psalm 32: 1-2, 5, 11
- 1 Corinthians 10: 31 – 11: 1
- Mark 1: 40-45

Today Catholic Christians celebrate the Sixth Sunday in Ordinary Time.

In today's reading from Leviticus, we hear how lepers were treated in those ancient days. They were shunned or excluded from other people and had to proclaim themselves "unclean" wherever they went.

And in the Gospel reading, we hear how Jesus not only refused to shun a leper, but actually touched him and healed him. Specifically we read, "Moved with pity, [Jesus] stretched out his hand, touched him and said to him, 'I do will it. Be made clean'" (Mark 1: 41).

Whenever I think of leprosy, which today is known as Hansen's disease, I think of St. Damien, a priest who devoted his life to serving lepers on the island of Molokai in Hawaii.

Joseph De Veuster was born in Belgium in 1840. From a very early age, he was very religious.

When he grew up, he joined the Congregation of the Sacred Hearts of Jesus and Mary and took as his Religious name, Damien. Though his superiors didn't think he was a good candidate for the priesthood, he was ordained, thanks to special tutoring by his priest-brother.

Because he always had a desire to be a foreign missionary, Damien eventually was sent to Hawaii to take the place of his brother, who had become sick. Once in Hawaii, Damien volunteered to be assigned to a leper colony called Kaluapappa on the Island of Molokai.

There, as nearly everywhere in those days, lepers were treated terribly, and the cure for the disease was yet undiscovered. People with leprosy were brought to the island in cages, dumped overboard, and left either to drown or swim to shore. There were no physicians, nurses, medicines, or clinics for the people on Molokai.

When Fr. Damien first arrived at Kaluapappa, he was horrified by the disfigurement of the people's faces, their open sores, the sight of worms crawling out of their wounds, the stench of the wounds, and the like. As he became used to his surroundings, though, he began to invite the people to his house and treat them with dignity and respect and love.

In his first six months on the island, Fr. Damien had 400 people studying to become Catholic Christians, and he began to build orphanages, houses, and clinics on the island. He started Perpetual Adoration for the people. And even though he suffered bouts of depression, he never let it interfere with serving his people.

After pleading with his superiors to send another priest to help him, he discovered what countless other pastors in history have learned: not all priests are helpful. In Damien's case, there was so much friction between him and the other priest that the other priest left.

In time, Fr. Damien himself contacted leprosy. When he wrote to his mother about that, she promptly had a heart attack and died.

Finally, a priest by the name of Fr. Conrady came to help Fr. Damien. He was a writer, and he began to inform the newspapers in Honolulu about the tremendous needs of the people of Kaluapappa. Then action began to happen. The Bishop of Honolulu was embarrassed into helping Damien, and soon priests and religious Sisters came to help.

When he was 49 years old, Fr. Damien died and was buried with other lepers near his church of St. Philomena. Soon the whole world learned about Fr. Damien's death, and he became a hero throughout the world.

When Hawaii became the 50th State of the United States, it was allowed to erect two statues in the capital building in Washington, D.C. just like every other state. One of those statues was that of Fr. Damien.

On October 11, 2009, Pope Benedict XVI canonized Damien. St. Damien is a patron saint of people afflicted with Hansen's disease – leprosy.

The life of St. Damien is a reflection of the life of Jesus Christ, and it serves as an inspiration for all of us. Like Jesus and Damien, we should never shun others. That is why all people are to be welcomed in our Catholic parishes. That is why Catholic Christians are called to go out of their way to give what is called the "preferential option to the poor." That is why we are to forgive our enemies and love those who harm us. That is why we are called to be a faith of "inclusion" rather than "exclusion." That is why we are not to judge the holiness of another person.

As we continue our life journeys this week, let's take some time to examine our own lives. How do we show we are living the "inclusive" nature of Jesus? How do we show "exclusion?"

And that is the good news I have for you on this Sixth Sunday in Ordinary Time.

Story sources:
- Matthew and Margaret Bunson, "St. Damien of Molokai: Apostle of the Exiled," Huntington, IN: *Our Sunday Visitor*, 2009.
- Kus, Fr. Robert J., "Saint Damien of Molokai," in *Saintly Men of Nursing: 100 Amazing* Stories, Wilmington, NC: Red Lantern Press, 2017, pp. 55-57.

Chapter 30

7th Sunday in Ordinary Time – B

St. Martin de Porres

<u>Scripture:</u>

- Isaiah 43: 18-19, 21-22, 24b-25
- Psalm 41: 2-3, 4-5, 13-14
- 2 Corinthians 1: 18-22
- Mark 2: 1-12

Today Catholic Christians celebrate the Seventh Sunday in Ordinary Time.

In today's Psalm, we read that God is very pleased with those who help the lowly and the poor. In fact, God tells us he will bless those who do so in many ways. In the Gospel reading from Mark, we see how a group of men helped their friend who was sick find his way to the healing graces of Jesus.

Fortunately for us, Catholic Christianity through the ages has produced an abundance of spectacular role models who have devoted their lives to helping those less fortunate than themselves. One of my favorite such heroes is St. Martin de Porres.

Martin was born in Lima, Peru in 1579. His father was a Spanish grandee, and his mother was a freed black slave woman from Panama. Because Martin had a dark complexion, his father abandoned him and Martin's mother when Martin was eight years old.

Martin grew up in poverty in Lima. When he was just twelve years old, his mother apprenticed him to a barber-surgeon to learn that trade. He learned how to cut hair, draw blood, care for wounds, and administer medicines.

When he was fifteen, Martin joined the local Dominican friary to be a "lay helper." He actually wanted to become a foreign missionary and become a martyr, but that wasn't permitted. Therefore, he began to do severe bodily penances to serve the Lord.

He did not feel worthy even to be a lay brother in the Order. After nine years, though, the men of the friary convinced him to become a Religious Brother. They saw how devoted Martin was to care of the poor and the sick. They saw how he treated everyone with dignity and respect regardless of their race, color, or social status. He loved to care for the slaves brought from Africa and for beggars, as well as for his religious Brothers.

Martin had other duties in the friary besides nursing the sick. He did laundry, cooked, and kept track of the friary's funds. He even cared for animals that he loved. For example, he kept a hospital for stray dogs and cats at his sister's house. And when some of the other members of the friary complained about mice living in the kitchen, Martin made a deal with the mice: if they would leave, he would feed them at the back door. From that day on, according to reports, the mice never came back into the kitchen while Martin was there.

Martin helped found an orphanage and school for the children of Lima. When the friary was in debt, he pleaded with his superiors to sell him. He said, "I am only a poor mulatto. Sell me. I am the property of the order. Sell me." Naturally, the Order did not do so.

Martin raised money for young women who needed a dowry to get married, and served as a spiritual director to many. One of his friends was St. Rose of Lima.

Because of Martin's spectacular love and care for the poor and sick, God showered him with supernatural blessings. For example, sometimes the other friars saw Martin lifted into the air while in the ecstasy of prayer, and many people claimed that he had the gift of bilocation—being able to be in two different places at the same time. Sometimes God used him to perform instant cures for people, and often he had what some called "miraculous knowledge," knowing things without being taught them.

Martin also gently guided his brothers on the path to sanctity when they strayed. Once, for example, he chided his brothers for making a black man sweep the floor in exchange for their aid, although they had not made a white man do the same thing the day before.

When Martin died on November 3, 1639, thousands upon thousands of people came to his funeral. He was canonized in 1962, and his feast day is November 3rd. He is a patron saint of hairdressers and of people of mixed racial background like the former American President Obama.

The life of St. Martin de Porres reflects what we read in Scripture today. In the Psalm, for example, we read:

> Blessed is the one who has regard for the lowly and poor;
>> in the day of misfortune the Lord will deliver him.
> The Lord will keep and preserve him;
>> and make him blessed on earth,
>> and not give him over to the will of his enemies.
> The Lord will help him on his sickbed;
>> he will take away all his ailment when he is ill
>> (Psalm 41: 2-4).

As we continue our life journey this week, let's take some time out to reflect on how we help our brothers and sisters in need. How do we reflect Jesus and St. Martin of Porres in our lives?

And that is the good news I have for you on this Seventh Sunday in Ordinary Time.

Story sources:
- "St. Martin de Porres," in Sarah Fawcett Thomas (Revision Editor), *Butler's Lives of the Saints New Full Edition – November*, Collegeville, MN: Burns & Oates/The Liturgical Press, 1997, pp. 18-20.
- Kus, Fr. Robert J., "Saint Martin de Porres," in *Saintly Men of Nursing: 100 Amazing Stories*. Wilmington, NC: Red Lantern Press, 2017, pp. 181-183.

Chapter 31

8th Sunday in Ordinary Time – B

Showing Up

<u>Scripture:</u>

- Hosea 2: 16b, 17b, 21-22
- Psalm 103: 1-2, 3-4, 8 & 10, 12-13
- 2 Corinthians 3: 1b-6
- Mark 2: 18-22

Today Catholic Christians celebrate the Eighth Sunday in Ordinary Time.

In today's Gospel selection from St. Mark, we hear how the disciples of John and the Pharisees were accustomed to fasting. They wondered, therefore, why Jesus' disciples did not also fast. Jesus asked them, "Can the wedding guests fast while the bridegroom is with them? As long as they have the bridegroom with them they cannot fast. But the days will come when the bridegroom is taken away from them, and they will fast on that day" (Mark 2: 19-20).

To clarify his remarks, Jesus said, "No one sews a piece of unshrunken cloth on an old cloak. If he does, its fullness pulls away, the new from the old, and the tear gets worse. Likewise, no one pours new wine into old wineskins. Otherwise, the wine will burst the skins, and both the wine and the skins are ruined. Rather, new wine is poured into fresh wineskins" (Mark 2: 21-22).

Jesus' message today is that what works at one time does not necessarily work at another. Adapting one's behavior appropriately to the circumstances is an important part of change, and change is a necessary element of growth. And growth, as we know, is a central theme of Jesus and his command to us to build the kingdom of God, beginning right here on Earth.

But before pointing out Biblical principles we can glean from today's Scripture passages, let's look at a true story by Saralee Perel called, "Just Show Up."

Saralee is a newspaper columnist on Cape Cod, Massachusetts. She wears a neck brace and needs a cane to keep her balance when walking. But she does love to walk, and she can frequently be seen walking on Cape Cod.

One day, while walking in the woods near her house, she met a man who changed her life by teaching her a three-word lesson.

The man's name was Morris, and he seemed to be in his seventies or eighties. He told Saralee that he walked every day "rain or shine."

When he noticed that Saralee wore a neck brace and was holding on to a tree, Morris asked her, "So is it hard for you to get around here?"

"Sometimes," she replied. "Frankly, though, it's harder for me to get here than it is to actually walk here. And that has nothing to do with needing a brace or a cane. It has to do with my thinking."

Morris smiled and replied, "You get caught up in maybe-I-will, maybe-I-won't land. That is the problem."

Saralee laughed at that and admitted that was a perfect summary of what she often felt when faced with going for a walk.

Morris wisely told her that there was a solution to getting out of "maybe-I-will, maybe-I-won't land." That solution simply to adopt three words to live by: "Just show up."

When Saralee got home, she told her husband Bob about her encounter with Morris, and how Morris had given her a new slogan: "Just show up."

When Bob asked what Morris had meant, Saralee explained that whenever she thought about going for a walk, her brain would immediately begin dwelling on every single step it takes to get around to doing it. For example, she would think about having to find something to wear, taking a shower, getting things for safety, and the like. Morris's guidance was to get rid of those thoughts and "Just show up." Simply focusing on the goal bypasses worrying about the details.

Bob started practicing this new way of thinking also, and he too found it very freeing. Now, instead of getting overwhelmed at his computer with all the details he has to do, he began to skip thinking about how complex his tasks are and thinks about the big picture by saying, "Just show up."

What Saralee and Bob both found was that what might have worked in the past no longer works in the present. It is time for a new approach, "new wineskins" so to speak.

Saralee's story ties in perfectly with today's Gospel passage. Here are three biblical principles we can glean from the passage.

First, we are called to grow in the spiritual life as followers of Jesus Christ. Nothing in the Scriptures suggests that we stay in a rut and stop growing.

Second, growth means change. What might have worked at one time does not necessarily work at another. At one point in time, leeches were used to treat wounds; now we use antibiotics. At one time people used pen and paper to write, but that gave way to using typewriters, and that gave way to computers.   In the spiritual life, we are also called to change. While "My First Bible" was good for us as first graders, as adults we need something more sophisticated.   We need to give more of ourselves as we grow. We need to become more active in building the kingdom of God on earth.

And third, change is hard but necessary. If we don't change, we get left behind. Imagine where we would be today if our ancestors chose not to adopt electricity or cars or airplanes. Likewise, we need to get rid of old habits that may have worked once, but no longer work. We need new wineskins for new wine.

And that is the good news I have for you on this Eighth Sunday in Ordinary Time.

Story source: Jack Canfield, Mark Victor Hansen, and Amy Newmark (Eds.). *Chicken Soup for the Soul: Think Positive*, Cos Cob, CT: CSS Publishing, 2010, pp. 19-22.

Chapter 32

9th Sunday in Ordinary Time – B

St. Cornelius

Scripture:

- Deuteronomy 5: 12-15
- Psalm 81: 3-4, 5-6ab, 6c-8a, 10-11b
- 2 Corinthians 4: 6-11
- Mark 2: 23 – 3: 6

Today Catholic Christians celebrate the Ninth Sunday in Ordinary Time.

In today's Old Testament selection from the Book of Deuteronomy, we hear the Lord say, "Take care to keep holy the Sabbath day as the Lord, your God, commanded you. Six days you may labor and do all your work; but the seventh day is the Sabbath of the Lord, your God. No work may be done then…" (Deuteronomy 5:12-14). The Sabbath refers to Saturday, traditionally the seventh day of the week.

Then in the Gospel passage from Mark, we hear about the Sabbath in a different way. This time we hear how the disciples of Jesus picked heads of grain to eat as they walked through the fields. The Pharisees criticized Jesus and his disciples for this "work" on the Sabbath. Jesus replied, "The Sabbath was made for man, not man for the Sabbath. That is why the Son of Man is lord even of the Sabbath" (Mark 2: 27).

Then, we hear how Jesus once again "violated" the Sabbath when he cured a man with a withered hand on the Sabbath. Knowing how the Pharisees were watching him closely to criticize him once again, Jesus asked before performing the miracle, "Is it lawful to do good on the Sabbath rather than to do evil, to save life rather than to destroy it?" (Mark 2: 4). When Jesus proceeded to cure the man, the Pharisees became infuriated and began to plan Jesus' death.

Now although the Old Testament passage is specifically about the Sabbath and why we should keep it holy, the passage from Mark is more about a spiritual disorder called rigorism. Rigorist persons put the "letter of the law" ahead of the "spirit of the law." Rigorists have always been present in the 2,000-year history of the Catholic Church.

Today we look at an early Church leader who fought against rigorism. His name was Cornelius.

In Cornelius' time, Pope St. Fabian died in January 250 during a violent persecution of the Church by the Roman Emperor Decius. The man most favored to succeed Fabian was a priest named Moses. Unfortunately, at the time the papacy was open, Fr. Moses was in prison. So the priests of Rome decided to put off electing a new pope. For 14 months, a college of clergy of Rome – led by a priest named Novatian – ran the Church.

130

But Fr. Moses died, so Fr. Novatian assumed he would become the new pope. However, Fr. Cornelius was also a contender. Though he seemed to be less qualified than Novatian to be pope, Cornelius had two qualities that the majority of the priests liked. First, he took the soft-line or pastoral view about lapsed Catholics returning to the Church. Second, he enjoyed the support of the powerful bishop of Carthage in Africa, St. Cyprian.

Novatian, on the other hand, believed that the Christians who had left the Church out of fear during the Decian persecution should be excommunicated. Cornelius believed that if they were repentant and did penance, they should be forgiven and welcomed back. Cornelius, as the majority favorite, was elected pope.

Incidentally, Novatian was not a gracious loser. In fact, after becoming consecrated as a bishop, he formed a sect outside the Church. In the year 251, a synod of 60 bishops came to Rome, and one of their acts was to excommunicate Novatian and his followers. Novatian's sect survived into the fifth century and then disappeared.

The life of St. Cornelius is very interesting in itself. But it is also a good example of the battle between rigorism and pastoralism that continues to this very day in the Catholic Church.

Rigorists, like the Pharisees of Jesus' day, tend to see the world in terms of black and white, despising shades of grey. Though they don't say it, they often act as though the Church was a "house of cards," and if one card is removed, the whole thing will crumble. For them, "truth" and protecting "the truth" seem to be paramount, and they view as "heretics" anyone who departs from their version of the "truth." Frequently these are angry and hostile persons, and they have no problem doing battle with anyone who does not agree with them. In the Protestant world, such people are known as "fundamentalists."

Pastoralists, on the other hand, are like Pope Cornelius and our own Pope Francis. Pastoralists focus on virtues such as kindness, joy, and welcome, and less on laws and rules and rubrics. For the pastoralist, rules are meant to be guides to serve people; people are not meant to worship rules. Pastoralists tend to be inclusive rather than exclusive, and they go out of their way to welcome the stranger. Love is the primary motivation of the pastoralist.

From reading the Scriptures, especially those about Jesus, I think it is crystal clear that leaders should be pastoral rather than rigoristic. Rules and regulations come and go, and teachings of the Church can change by the workings of the Holy Spirit. The Catholic Church is alive, for the Spirit is alive. That is why we occasionally revise the Church's catechism, for a catechism is merely a snapshot of the belief system of the Church at a given point in history.

As we continue our life journeys this week, it would be good to reflect on the priests we have known. Though most priests have elements of both tendencies, each leans more toward one pole or the other. Which ones leaned in the pastoral direction, and which tended to be a rigorist? What makes you say that?

And that is the good news I have for you on this Ninth Sunday in Ordinary Time.

Story source: "St. Cornelius," *Butler's Lives of the Saints: New Full Edition: September*, Revised by Sarah Fawcett Thomas. Collegeville, MN: Burns & Oates/The Liturgical Press, 1999, p. 137-139.

Chapter 33

10th Sunday in Ordinary Time – B

A House Divided

Scripture:

- Genesis 3: 9-15
- Psalm 130: 1-2, 3-4, 5-6ab and 7a, 7b-8
- 2 Corinthians 4: 13 – 5: 1
- Mark 3: 20-35

Today Catholic Christians celebrate the Tenth Sunday in Ordinary Time.

In today's Gospel selection from St. Mark (3: 20-35), we hear the story of certain Scribes, Jewish legal scholars of the day, who tried to minimize Jesus' healing ministry and popularity by demonizing his work. They claimed, for example, that Beelzebub – a demonic Philistine god – had taken possession of Jesus. Furthermore, they claimed that Jesus drove out demons by the prince of demons.

Jesus spoke to the illogical conclusions of his enemies by saying, "How can Satan drive out Satan? If a kingdom is divided against itself, that kingdom cannot stand. And if a house is divided against itself, that house will not be able to stand. And if Satan has risen up against himself and is divided, he cannot stand; that is the end of him" (Mark 3: 23b-26).

These words of wisdom are as relevant today as they were in the time Jesus walked on the Earth. Jesus was actually singing the praises of unity, for only in unity can a group be strong.

In our own country, for example, we hear Jesus' words echoed in the famous speech by a young politician from Illinois who was running for President of the United States of America in 1858. The man's name was Abraham Lincoln,

At the time of this speech, there was great turmoil in the United States. States of the North were for freedom of all people, while States of the South were for freedom only for whites.

On June 16, 1858, Abraham Lincoln gave one of the most powerful and famous speeches ever given by a politician. It came to be known as the "House Divided Speech." In part, it echoed Jesus' words.

Abraham Lincoln said, in part:

A house divided against itself cannot stand. I believe this government cannot endure, permanently, half slave and half free. I do not expect the Union to be dissolved—I do not expect the house to fall—but I do expect it will cease to be divided. It will become all one thing or all the other. Either the opponents of slavery will arrest the further spread of it, and place it where the public mind shall rest in the belief that it is in the course of ultimate extinction; or its advocates will push it forward, till it shall become lawful in all the States, old as well as new— North as well as South.

This speech by Abraham Lincoln sowed the seeds of freedom for all those enslaved because of their skin color. Eventually, as we know, the United States of America would one day abolish slavery, and all people would come to be seen as free, as equal citizens of the nation. Though it took a grievous civil war and a great deal of time, people would one day be granted equal rights under the law on the basis of race and skin color, and eventually sexual orientation. Indeed we are still waiting for equality of gender, for there are still laws on the books that continue to treat men and women unequally.

Today, we explore the idea of unity in the Church. As we will see, unity is a fine idea, but it is not an absolute value.

In discussing the idea of unity in the Church, St. Augustine noted that in essentials, we should have unity; in doubtful things, we should have liberty; and in all things, we should show charity. Let's look at each of these principles.

First, what does it mean to have "unity in essentials?" It means we all need to know what are the "essentials" of our Faith and assent to them. The "essentials" are the "non-negotiable" teachings of our Faith. Among these essentials are our beliefs that there is only one God; that in God there are Three Divine Persons – Father, Son, and Holy Spirit; that Jesus is the Savior; that God created the universe; and the like. These beliefs will never change. To help us remember the "essentials" of the Faith, we have creeds – such as the Nicene Creed – that we say each at each Sunday liturgy.

Second, what does it mean to say that in "doubtful things" we are to have liberty? Well, liberty means freedom, and "doubtful things" means ideas or beliefs that are not "essentials" of the faith. In these non-essentials, Catholic Christians can and do question such beliefs. In the 2,000-year history of Catholic Christianity, there have crept into the Faith many ideas that are not Biblical or essential to the Faith. For example, some people believe that Mary has appeared to people in trees or grottos or other places. Whether she did or didn't is debatable. Marian appearances are not "essentials" of our Faith.

But third, in all things, whether essentials or non-essentials, we are to exercise the crown jewel of all virtues – charity, also known as love. Lamentably, this is all too frequently absent in religious discussions. Instead of discussing issues and being respectful of others' opposite opinions, some people attack opponents rather than their ideas. This is not in harmony with the triple-love commandment of Jesus Christ – the commandment that requires us to love God, our neighbors, as we love our self.

As we continue our life journeys this week, it would be a good idea to reflect on how we view unity in the Church, and how we view the freedom to disagree in non-essentials of our Faith.

And that is the good news I have for you on this Tenth Sunday in Ordinary Time.

Chapter 34

11th Sunday in Ordinary Time – B

The Power of Mark

Scripture:

- Ezekiel 17: 22-24
- Psalm 92: 2-3, 13-14, 15-16
- 2 Corinthians 5: 6-10
- Mark 4: 26 - 34

Today Catholic Christians celebrate the Eleventh Sunday in Ordinary Time.

In today's Gospel selection from St. Mark, we hear two parables from Jesus describing the kingdom of God.

In the first parable, Jesus talks about how a farmer scatters seeds. Even when the farmer is sleeping, the seeds grow until the day they become a plant. Then, the farmer is able to harvest them.

In the second parable, Jesus describes the Kingdom of God as "like a mustard seed that, when it is sown in the ground, is the smallest of all seeds on earth. But once it is sown, it springs up and becomes the largest of plants and puts forth large branches, so that the birds of the sky can dwell in its shade" (Mark 4: 31-32).

The theme of both parables is, of course, growth. Like the mustard seed, we too must grow and flourish.

Before examining some Biblical principles that we can glean from this passage, let's look at a story by Phil Bauer called, "The Power of Mark." It shows how a father grew and, in the process, became a much freer person.

Phil and his wife Cookie had two sons, Brian and Mark. Brian and Mark were less than two years apart in age, Brian being the older of the two. Like their parents, they were very close to one another. But as they came to their teenage years, the brothers developed different interests and identities.

Unlike his brother, Mark grew withdrawn and quiet.

Like all teens, Mark struggled with various adolescent issues. His parents believed, however, that he had successfully met his challenges and successfully conquered them as he went from a skinny little kid to a 5-foot, 9-inch, 175-pound young man.

As Mark neared his high school graduation, it appeared that his teenage problems had disappeared. Then, on Friday, May 28, 2004, tragedy struck the Bauer home. Mark never woke up. He had taken a mix of prescription drugs that didn't belong to him, and died from an overdose.

For Mark's father, Phil, all joy and happiness left that day. Nothing seemed important to him anymore except his wife Cookie and his son Brian.

Phil was consumed with heartache, sadness, feelings of emptiness, and bitterness. He no longer smiled or laughed. Because of his negative presentation of self, his friends gradually abandoned him.

Phil, who had previously audited hospitals and government agencies, lost interest in his work. Soon, he was without a job, and without a job he no longer had an income or health insurance. Finally, though, he was faced with reality; he needed a new career.

The only thing Phil felt passionate about was telling others about the dangers of substance abuse. But he had no formal training in that field, nor did he have training in public speaking or education.

One day, Phil came to the realization that he had something amazing, something he called "The Power of Mark." This "power" allowed him to become free from phobias and to become honest with others and with himself. This "power" gave Phil the courage to do things he could not have done before.

So, what was this miraculous "Power of Mark?" Well, previous to Mark's death, Phil's life was characterized by certain self-limiting principles: don't make waves; accept "no" for an answer; know your place; understand your limitations; fear failure; understand organizational "hierarchy;" respect others because of their status; and the like. And indeed one of Phil's biggest fears was speaking in front of groups because of a fear of failure. If he knew he had to talk in front of a group, he would not be able to sleep the night before.

Then, one day, he realized he had the "Power of Mark." This meant that he came to realize that the loss of his son was the worst thing that could have happened to him. He realized that nothing could hurt him more, so why should he be afraid? Why should he care what other people think? In other words, he now had a new power, a new freedom. This new nature was "The Power of Mark."

Today, Brian has no problem devoting his life to speaking to conferences and individuals about the dangers of substance abuse. He freely talks about Mark and Mark's death, and what it was like as a father to endure that.

Phil, out of tragedy, grew and flourished, just as the seeds Jesus talked about in today's parables grew and flourished.

Here are three Biblical principles we can glean from the Scriptures and the story of Phil.

First, we are all called to grow and flourish, for such is the Kingdom of God.

Second, growth involves change, and change is often difficult. It is more comfortable to stay in a rut than to move into uncharted territories of the paths of our life journeys.

And third, growth can not only produce expected changes, it can also bring us unexpected blessings, as Phil experienced when changes in his life brought him freedom.

Today as we continue our life journeys, it would be a good idea to reflect on our life. How are we growing? What things are preventing us from growing more fully?

And that is the good news I have for you on this Eleventh Sunday in Ordinary Time.

Story source: Phil Bauer, "The Power of Mark," in Jack Canfield, Mark Victor Hansen and Amy Newmark (Eds.), *Chicken Soup for the Soul: Think Positive*, Cos Cob, CT: Chicken Soup for the Soul Publishing, 2010, pp. 331-333.

Chapter 35

12th Sunday in Ordinary Time – B

The Trouble Tree

<u>Scripture:</u>

- Job 38: 1, 8-11
- Psalm 107: 23-24, 25-26, 28-29, 30-31
- 2 Corinthians 5: 14-17
- Mark 4: 35-41

Today Catholic Christians celebrate the Twelfth Sunday in Ordinary Time.

On this day, we hear the fascinating story of Jesus and his disciples in a boat on a stormy sea (Mark 4: 35-41). While Jesus slept on a large pillow, the disciples were terrified that the boat would capsize. When they woke up Jesus, he calmly commanded the sea, "Quiet! Be still!" Suddenly, the sea was calm once again. When Jesus discovered how fearful the disciples were, he asked, "Why are you terrified? Do you not yet have faith?" (Mark 4: 40).

Oftentimes we are like the disciples. We are surrounded by the storms of life, and we are afraid. We fail to trust that God is with us.

In the following story, we see how one man, a carpenter, developed an interesting strategy to cope with the storms of his life.

There was once a carpenter who had a very bad day. He lost an hour of pay because of a flat tire, his electric saw quit working, and his old truck refused to start at the end of the day.

While his foreman drove him home, he sat in stony silence, fuming with anger. When they got to his home, the carpenter invited his boss to come into the house to meet his family. But before getting to the house, the carpenter paused briefly at a large pine tree in his front yard and touched the tips of the branches with both hands.

When he opened the front door, he underwent an amazing transformation. His tanned face glowed with smiles, and he gave hugs to his two small children and a long embrace and kiss to his wife. After a while, he walked his boss back to his car. As they passed the pine tree, the foreman's curiosity got the better of him. He asked the carpenter about the "tree ritual" that he had seen him do earlier.

"Oh, that's my trouble tree," he replied. "I know I can't help having troubles on the job. However, one thing for sure is that I should never bring my troubles and frustrations into the home at the end of the day. So, I stop by that pine tree over there and visualize hanging on it whatever troubles, frustrations and worries I have." The carpenter then smiled and said, "You know, a funny thing happens when I come out in the morning to pick them up again. There aren't nearly as many as I remember hanging on the tree the night before."

142

This story is a good example of how an ordinary man coped with the ordinary troubles of everyday life in an odd but mature way. As a result of the way he chose to cope with life's problems, he and his family both benefited tremendously. Unlike the disciples who were terrified in the storm, this man's approach was mature and confident. He did not "go to pieces" emotionally.

From the stories of Jesus calming the storm and the carpenter's trouble tree, we can glean at least three points.

First, everyone has problems in everyday life. There are no exceptions. Though we may not always have troubles as severe as being on a sinking boat or having swathe tools of our trade stop working, we always have a host of smaller problems. Many people, for example, have credit card debt they can't pay. Others are plagued with an unreasonable boss or obnoxious coworkers. Others may have constant fatigue from trying to juggle too many adult social roles. Others may constantly battle obesity.

Second, we know there are two main ways to approach our life problems. One way is the mature path. That is the method chosen by the carpenter. Instead of taking his anger out on his family, he developed a clever strategy of symbolically putting his troubles on his "trouble tree," making him kind and cheerful with his family.

But often we act in less mature, less effective, even counter-productive ways. People may try to forget the worry of their credit card debt by going on a shopping spree. They may stay in dead-end jobs instead of going to school to open up their occupational horizons, or simply looking for a new place to work. Some may deal their constant exhaustion by adding more and more responsibilities to their lives because they can't say "no."

Third, we can learn from the Gospel story that God is always with us. Sometimes we forget that. We think we are alone. We get fearful. We panic and lash out at others. We often go around in circles searching for earthly solutions.

Jesus tells his disciples to have faith when they find themselves in a storm. That is very hard for many of us if we don't understand the big picture, God's plan for us. We sometimes forget that God is "on the job" watching over us always.

As we continue our life journeys this week, it would be a good idea to ask ourselves some questions. What are my biggest problems? How am I handling them? Am I facing my problems maturely or immaturely? Am I making my problems worse by how I pretend to deal with them? Do I call on God to help me?

And that is the good news I have for you on this Twelfth Sunday in Ordinary Time.

Story source: Anonymous, "The Trouble Tree," in Brian Cavanaugh (Ed.), *Sower's Seeds that Nurture Family Values: Sixth Planting.* New York: Paulist Press, 2000, #4, pp. 9-10.

Chapter 36

13th Sunday in Ordinary Time – B

The Faithful Old Well

<u>Scripture:</u>

- Wisdom 1: 13-15; 2: 23-24
- Psalm 30: 2 & 4, 5-6, 11 & 12a & 13b
- 2 Corinthians 8: 7, 9, 13-15
- Mark 5: 21-43

Today Catholic Christians celebrate the Thirteenth Sunday in Ordinary Time.

On this day, we hear about two important Christian principles: generosity and equality. In the Gospel Jesus uses his healing powers to give health and life to a woman who had suffered from hemorrhages for twelve years and to the daughter of a government official (Mark 5: 21-43).

In Paul's second letter to the Corinthians, we hear how Christians are to give of their abundance to achieve equality among people. Paul says, "For you know the gracious act of our Lord Jesus Christ, that though he was rich, for your sake he became poor, so that by his poverty you might become rich. Not that abundance at the present time should supply their needs, so that their abundance may also supply your needs, that there may be equality. As it is written: *Whoever had much did not have more, and whoever had little did not have less*" (2 Corinthians 8: 9, 13-15).

Generosity is not a suggestion for the Christian. It is a commandment of Jesus Christ. When we practice generosity of our time, talent, and treasure, God showers us with more abundance. However, when we fail to be generous, we find that we must struggle with obtaining what we want. That is what we see in the following story by John Sanford.

There was once a young boy who went each summer for a month-long vacation to an old farmhouse owned by his parents. The house was 150 years old and had never been modernized, so the water for the house came from an old well just outside the front door of the house. Every summer, the family could count on the old faithful well to provide them water. Even in summers when there was a severe drought, the old well provided cool, clear water.

One summer, though, the family decided to modernize the old farmhouse. They had a new well dug a few hundred feet from the house, and capped the old well to keep in reserve.

The old well remained covered for several years. One day, moved by curiosity, the son, now a young man, decided to uncover and inspect the old well. When he uncovered the well, he expected the same cool water that he had remembered as a boy. But instead it was bone dry.

146

He consulted a professor at the local university to learn why the well, faithful for so many years, had dried up. The professor told the young man that this type of well is fed by hundreds of tiny underground rivulets along which constant trickle of water seeps. As water is drawn from the well, more water flows into these rivulets, keeping the tiny channels clear and open. But when such a well is not used regularly, the tiny rivulets close up. The well that had worked so generously for so many years was now dry simply because it had not been used.

Generosity is a theme that we find throughout both the Old and New Testaments of the Bible. In the New Testament, for example, we hear how the more generous we are, the more God will bless us. Entrepreneurs—people who start their own businesses—learn this lesson very quickly, or they go out of business. Christian financial advisors also are very well aware of this principle. In fact, the first thing Christian financial advisors encourage people to do when facing bankruptcy is to begin tithing to their church, if they are not already doing so. They know first-hand that wealth is a flowing process. The more wealth flows, the more it grows and is replenished.

But while we Christians all know how God will bless us in relation to how generous we are, today we hear something related that we often gloss over or ignore in the Scripture. That principle is called equality, and it is found in today's second letter of St. Paul to the Corinthians.

In this letter, Paul not only reminds the early Christians to be generous with their abundance, but to do so to achieve equality among themselves. We hear this same principle stated in the Acts of the Apostles when we learn that the early Christians gave all they had to the Apostles. The Apostles, in turn, gave to each individual according to their need. Thus, there was no distinction of poor and rich among the early Christians. They practiced a form of Christian socialism, a striving to treat all people as equal.

Today we are the Christians two thousand years away from the early disciples. Are we still called to be generous? Of course. Do we always practice generosity? Unfortunately, we often do not. We sometimes become clouded by materialism, by greed, by selfishness. Christ's commandment of generosity, however, still stands.

Do we treat all people as equal? Unfortunately, we often do not.
Societies and even religions, including our own, continue to value some
people more than others. We divide people on the basis of their wealth,
occupation, gender, sexual orientation, age, skin color, country of birth,
neighborhood, health, looks, and many other factors. But as
discouraging as this news is, the good news is that we can always keep
trying. Christians can always strive to be more generous and strive for
equality of all peoples in the days and years to come.

And that is the good news I have for you on this Thirteenth
Sunday in Ordinary Time.

Story source: John Sanford, "The Old Faithful Well," in Brian Cavanaugh (Ed.), *Sower's Seeds of Encouragement: Fifth Planting,* New York: Paulist Press, 1998, #15, pp. 14-15.

Chapter 37

14th Sunday in Ordinary Time – B

St. John Vianney

<u>Scripture:</u>

- Ezekiel 2: 2-5
- Psalm 123: 1-2a, 2bcd, 3-4
- 2 Corinthians 12: 7-10
- Mark 6: 1-6

Today Catholic Christians celebrate the Fourteenth Sunday in Ordinary Time.

In today's reading from St. Paul's second letter to the Corinthians, we hear how God works his power through the weakness of his disciples. Paul reports how God gave him a "thorn in the flesh" and that he begged God three times to remove it. Instead of removing the unwanted "thorn," God told Paul, "My grace is sufficient for you, for power is made perfect in weakness" (2 Corinthians 12: 9). Once Paul understood this, he rejoiced in his weakness.

Many Bible scholars have speculated what this "thorn in the side" actually was. Some think it might have been a physical illness. Others think it may have been a personality characteristic that Paul did not like. Others speculate that it was an emotional difficulty. Nobody knows for sure what the "thorn in the flesh" was. It is not important. The important thing is that we learn a very important Biblical principle in this reading, namely, that God works through human weakness to achieve his goals.

That is indeed good news, for all of us have weaknesses. It also goes a long way in helping us understand why God chooses the people he does to lead his Church. When we look at the type of people God chooses as priests and other ministers, we are often baffled at how they were chosen, because of their many flaws. But when we realize God has a plan for working through weakness, God's choices make more sense.

One great example of a man with many flaws that God chose to be a priest was John Vianney.

John was born into a very religious French Catholic family on May 8, 1786 and baptized on the same day. He grew up with five siblings in rural France. His parents were noted for their generosity towards the poor. In fact, one day the family provided hospitality to St. Benedict Joseph Labré who went on to become the patron saint of tramps.

Because of the French Revolution, many Catholic priests had to conduct Mass in secrecy. The Vianney family continued to attend Mass even though it was illegal. Young John began to see the priests as heroes, doing their work illegally. Some nuns privately gave John sacramental preparation, and he was able to receive his First Communion and Confirmation.

150

Though he learned how to read and write, his educational background was very weak. When John was nineteen, his father allowed him to leave the farm and be tutored by a parish priest so that John could one day be ordained. Unfortunately, the priest taught in Latin, and most of John's classmates were boys of eleven and twelve. John's poor educational background prevented him from mastering the academic material.

John's studies were interrupted by a call to the army, but for a number of reasons, he never did serve in the military. In fact, he lived as a deserter for many months.

Finally John was ordained in 1815, even though the Church authorities did not think much of this "slow" priest. After serving a little while with his mentor, Fr. John was sent to the little town of Ars, a place where the Church authorities believed he could not do too much harm.

Fr. John preached on the basis of the theology that was common in France in those days. The focus was on evil and eternal damnation instead of God's love and mercy. Fr. John was highly specific in his sermons. In fact, they were so specific, that today he would most likely be removed from active ministry. For example, he not only told the people about the evils of swearing, he told the people in his sermons all the bad words they should avoid.

He also performed personal physical mortifications that were seen as virtuous in those days. Today such acts would more likely be seen as signs of imprudence and pride, and a violation of God's triple love commandment.

John's main ministry, though, was celebrating Reconciliation, and it is for this that he became well known. In fact, thousands of people flocked to Ars to go to confession with this priest. In the winter, he would often hear confessions for eleven hours a day, and on summer days he would spend as much as sixteen hours in the confessional.

Because of his lifestyle, John tried to run away from his parish, but the people always dragged him back.

He was canonized a saint in 1925 and declared to be the patron saint of parish priests. His feast day is August 4.

How great it is that God can work wonders through those who have so many shortcomings. In fact, it is through shortcomings that God's greatest works often occur. A great question to ponder for this coming week would be: What kind of shortcomings does God use in my life to work his wonders?

And that is the good news I have for you on this Fourteenth Sunday in Ordinary Time.

Story source: "St. John Vianney," in John Cumming (Revision Editor), *Butler's Lives of the Saints, New Full Edition - August*, Collegeville, MN: Burns & Oates/The Liturgical Press, 1998, pp. 28-33.

Chapter 38

15th Sunday in Ordinary Time – B

Parish Twinning

<u>Scripture:</u>

- Amos 7: 12-15
- Psalm 85: 9ab & 10, 11-12, 13-14
- Ephesians 1: 3-14
- Mark 6: 7-13

Today Catholic Christians celebrate the Fifteenth Sunday in Ordinary Time.

In today's Gospel reading, we hear how Jesus sent out his Apostles as missionaries two by two. From our baptism, we too are called to be missionaries. Most of us do that by acting as "living homilies," that is, living in such a way that others are attracted to us by our Christ-centered lives. This is called being "lights to the world."

There are, though, other ways of living the missionary mandate of Jesus Christ. One of the ways that many Catholic Americans partially fulfill their missionary mandate is to engage in what is known as "parish twinning."

Parish twinning refers to a typical American parish "adopting" another parish, usually in a different country, which is much poorer than the American parish. Both parishes agree to pray for each other and to keep in contact. In addition, the American parish agrees to help support the poorer parish. Usually this is done by sending money to the sister parish from second collections, and sometimes it involves sending material things needed by the poorer parish. For its part, the foreign sister parish agrees to host lay missionaries from the American parish who seek to assist in the parish's work, while learning more about the Church in another society. Thus, both parishes benefit. Let's take the example of our own parish of the Basilica Shrine of St. Mary in Wilmington, NC and its sister parish of San Francisco de Asís Parish in Reitoca, FM, Honduras.

St. Mary Parish is an American parish of approximately 6,000 parishioners. It offers six weekend Masses, four in English and two in Spanish. In the congregation are people from every continent of the world except Antarctica. Only five percent of the people come from North Carolina. Most of the congregation comes from North America, especially Mexico and the northern states of the USA. The parish is financially sound and has a strong tradition of helping the poor.

Unlike most American parishes, which have just one church facility in one location, parishes in many other nations have many houses of worship. Such is the case of San Francisco de Asís, a very poor mountain parish in the Archdiocese of Tegucigalpa, FM, Honduras. [FM stands for Francisco Morazán, the name of the *Departamento*—which is

154

like a state—in which Tegucigalpa and St. Mary's sister parish are located.] The main town of the parish is called Reitoca.

San Francisco de Asís Parish has 87 churches and chapels with about 50,000 Catholics. To serve all these parishioners, there are only two ordained priests. It takes four hours by jeep or pickup truck to get to many of the churches. Some of the churches are accessible only by burro or horse and walking, and it can take six hours to reach these places. There are five "*municipios*" or larger towns in the parish, each serving as a hub of several other churches of the parish. The priests try to provide at least one Mass in each of the five *municipios* each weekend. Needless to say, most of the churches do not get to have a Mass very often.

Specially trained lay people called *Delegados de la Palabra* (delegates of the Word) run the little churches on a daily basis. They also conduct home rituals with their people, including wake services for the dead and *Quinceañeras* for fifteen-year old girls. They also conduct a Liturgy of the Word service every Thursday evening in their little churches. In the United States they would be more like Pastoral Administrators.

Helping the *Delegados* are *Catequistas* who pass on the Faith through education. They also prepare children and youth for sacraments of initiation (Baptism, Confirmation, and First Communion).

Some of the churches of the parish have Religious Sisters who serve in many capacities.

Until a month or two ago, San Francisco parish had only one priest, but now it has two. The Pastor's pay is $50 per month. Much of his life is spent traveling in his pickup truck, driving on unpaved mountain roads.

The people are, for the most part, very poor. Because this is a very rural parish, most of the people work in agriculture. In the towns, people also have little "*tiendas*" or stores, in their homes. Unfortunately, because so many have these little stores, they are not able to make much money from them.

Health care is usually a luxury for most people. In Reitoca, however, the people have Clínica Santa María that whose existence was made possible by donations from the Basilica Shrine of St. Mary parishioners. Most parts of the far-flung parish, however, have no health care services.

In some of the churches of the parish, there is no electricity or running water, so a lot of time in everyday life is spent struggling to meet basic needs. One fourteen-year old boy I encountered on my visit to this parish had to walk three hours—one way—to get to a store to buy food for his family of ten. Then he had to walk back home—three hours—carrying the food. This was not an unusual occurrence for him.

Despite all the difficulties the people of this 87-church parish face, they have a wonderful resilience and deep faith. When they hear that the priest is coming to celebrate a Mass in their local church, they come to church. Many of them walk two hours—one way—on dusty mountain roads and trails to get to Mass.

Fortunately, St. Mary's has been able to make life a little easier for the Pastor and his parish. Parishioners are now able to accomplish little projects - that could not be done before - because of American money. Lay missionaries from St. Mary's are able to have a life-changing experience in another country that is so near, yet so far away.

And that is the good news I have for you on this Fifteenth Sunday in Ordinary Time.

Chapter 39

16th Sunday in Ordinary Time – B

The Wordy Preacher

<u>Scripture:</u>

- Jeremiah 23: 1-6
- Psalm 23: 1-3a, 3b-4, 5, 6
- Ephesians 2: 13-18
- Mark 6: 30-34

Today Catholic Christians celebrate the Sixteenth Sunday in Ordinary Time.

On this day, we hear the theme of shepherding.   In the Old Testament reading from the Prophet Jeremiah, for example, we hear how shepherds are not to scatter the flock.   Rather, they are to keep the herd safe and sound and unified.   We then hear part of the Twenty-Third Psalm, the favorite psalm for many people, which compares the Lord to a shepherd who is always by our side.   Finally, in the Gospel reading from Mark we see Jesus' heart moved with pity as he saw so many people flocking to hear him.   In fact, he compared them to "sheep without a shepherd."

Certainly good shepherds are necessary.   We need religious leaders to guide us in the Faith.   However, we must always remember that God speaks through all his people, not only through officials.   In other words, while professional or academic leadership is good and necessary, there is also another dimension of shepherding that involves the heart rather than the mind.   This important principle, often totally overlooked by academics in seminaries and among the clergy, can be seen in the following story.

There was once an excellent preacher.   One day, he met a very intellectual man who was not a Christian.   The preacher invited the man to his church, and for the next several weeks, he preached a series of homilies on some very challenging Scripture passages.   The preacher did his absolute best in the hopes that the intellectual man would one day become a Christian.   And indeed after the series of homilies, the man came to the preacher and announced his intentions to become a Christian and join the preacher's church.   Naturally, the preacher was delighted.

Pleased with himself, the preacher said, "And which of my homilies was it that removed your doubts?"   The man replied, "Your homilies?   Oh, it wasn't any of your homilies."

The preacher, greatly disappointed that it was not his homilies that brought the man to Jesus, asked, "What was it then that led you to become a Christian?"

The man said, "The thing that began to make me think of coming to Christ happened one day when I was coming out of the church.

There was a poor woman who stumbled down the stairs right beside me. When I put out my hand to help her, she smiled and said, 'Thank you.' She then added, 'Do you love Jesus Christ, my blessed Savior? He means everything to me.' I thought much about what she said. I realized that I had been on the wrong road in my search. I had been trying to find Jesus with my head, when all along, I should have been trying to find Jesus with my heart. I still have many questions, but now Jesus means everything to me, too."

This story is not only an inspirational one, it is also very important. It challenges all of us to stop and look at our own Faith journey. Catholic Christians, especially, need to stop and take stock of their spiritual lives when hearing such a story.

Catholic Christianity places a high priority on academics. We start universities and require many years of study for men to become priests. We take great stock in scholars such as St. Thomas Aquinas. In the United States, a third of all doctorates granted by our universities go to Catholic Christians, even though we only make up one-fourth of the population.

In our liturgies, we also tend to be very methodical and reserved. Unlike many branches of Christianity that have highly emotional services, our worship seems rather dull. We often put head above heart.

But when we stop and reflect on the story of the man in the above story, we are forced to stop for a minute. To whom do we look as models of Faith?

I have asked myself that question, and I have come to some interesting conclusions.

On the one hand, I am very grateful for the wonderful education I have. My academic background in sociology, psychiatric-mental health nursing, writing, and priesthood help me every day in my ministry as a priest. I treasure scholarship and academic excellence. I am able to identify and classify various religious experiences, discuss the types of spirituality common in Catholic Christianity, talk about Church history, the Bible, liturgy, current issues in the Church, and a host of other things.

But on the other hand, when I look for examples of holiness and models of Faith, I look not to religious leaders, but rather to the people I encounter in everyday life. In prayer, for example, I admire a poor man who can barely read or write, has only a second grade education, makes the Sign of the Cross backwards, and yet puts his whole heart and soul thanking God for all the many blessings he has.

I look to people who have little in the way of material things yet come to St. Mary's filled with joy and gratitude. Those are the kind of people who touch my core, the center where Jesus lives.

So, who touches your Faith life? Who touches your heart? Who gives you examples of Faith that you want to emulate in your life?

And that is the good news I have for you on this Sixteenth Sunday in Ordinary Time.

Story source: Anonymous, "Story of the Wordy Preacher," in *God's Little Devotional Book for Men*, Tulsa, OK: Honor Books, 1996, p. 9.

Chapter 40

17th Sunday in Ordinary Time – B

Sharing the Bread

<u>Scripture:</u>

- 2 Kings 4: 42-44
- Psalm 145: 10-11, 15-16, 17-18
- Ephesians 4: 1-6
- John 6: 1-15

Today Catholic Christians celebrate the Seventeenth Sunday in Ordinary Time.

On this day, we hear what many call "Eucharistic stories." In the Old Testament reading from Second Kings, for example, we hear how God fed one hundred people with only twenty barley loaves. Not only did he feed them, but there was bread left over. And in the Gospel reading, we hear how the disciples were able to feed thousands of people with just five loaves and a couple of fish that Jesus had blessed. Not only did the blessed food feed the multitudes, there was enough left over to fill twelve basketsful.

These stories foreshadow the Last Supper when Jesus took bread and wine and turned them into his Body and Blood and gave the command to his disciples to continue this practice. For two thousand years, Catholic Christians have continued to celebrate the Eucharist, or Mass, faithfully. And like the stories we hear today, there is never an end to God's graciousness in providing us with the "manna from heaven" in the Eucharist.

In Catholic Christianity, the Eucharist is so important that the Church leaders at the Second Vatican Council called it the "source and summit" of our spirituality. And because it is so important, the Mass can be explored in an infinite number of ways. Today I would like to explore the concept of Eucharist in terms of sharing with others. This tradition is discussed in the current *Catechism of the Catholic Church* (C 1397) and in the First Letter of St. Paul to the Corinthians when he tells we are to care for the poorest members of the community (11: 17-34). In the following story, we hear about such sharing.

Dave Huebsch, who has been doing human development for several years in Guatemala, tells this story. One day, he and a Guatemalan companion were traveling on foot in the mountains carrying a heavy load. They stopped to rest under a mango tree amid cane houses in a tiny village. Pretty soon, curious children came to visit them. The children did not have things American children have such as swing sets, television, or coloring books. Rather, they came from houses made out of cane or corn stalks, houses with dirt floors. Dave told the children a story, a gift that they loved.

162

Dave and his companion then peeled and divided the oranges they had in their backpacks and gave them to the dozen or so children until only a half of an orange remained. This they gave to a very shy girl of seven. After thanking the two men, she broke the orange half into two pieces. She gave one half to her little brother, and the other half to her little sister. Then she thanked the men again and went off with nothing for herself.

A year later, Dave found himself in the same village visiting a family whose father was gravely ill. Sitting on the dirt floor of their smoky house made of cornstalks, Dave prayed for the father with the rest of the family—a mother and six children—until darkness came.

Then a little girl climbed into his lap. Dave wanted to reassure her that her dad would be okay, but he knew that the dad would probably not get better. He wanted to be able to tell her that her brothers and sisters would be able to go to school, that there would be plenty to eat.

But when he thought about eating, he remembered that he had some wheat buns in his backpack. He also knew that these poor families often went without eating, so he gave all but one of the buns to the mother of the family. Dave gave the last bun to the little girl on his lap. To his surprise, the child said thanks, took the bread, broke it, and gave it to her smaller brother and sister sitting beside them. And, though she had nothing for herself, she expected nothing more.

And that is how Dave recognized the little girl he had met the year before…in the way she said thanks, took the bread, broke it, and shared it.

This beautiful story reminds us that the Eucharist or Mass is not something that is detached from us. On the contrary, it should always be a source of change for us. We should never leave Mass as quite the same person we were when we entered it. Rather, we should be transformed. And among the many ways we should be transformed is to become more generous with what we have. Especially we should be generous to the poorest of the poor.

As we continue our life journeys this week, it would be a good idea to ask ourselves how the experience of Eucharist is making us more generous to those in need.

And that is the good news I have for you on this Seventeenth Sunday in Ordinary Time.

Story source: Dave Huebsch, "The Least of My Brothers," in Jack Canfield, Mark Victor Hansen, & LeAnn Thieman (Eds.), *Chicken Soup for the Soul: Living Catholic Faith*, Cos Cob, CT: CSS Publishing, 2008, pp. 70-71.

Chapter 41

18th Sunday in Ordinary Time – B

An Attitude of Gratitude

<u>Scripture:</u>

- Exodus 16: 2-4, 12-15
- Psalm 78: 3 & 4bc, 23-24, 25 & 54
- Ephesians 4: 17, 20-24
- John 6: 24-35

Today Catholic Christians celebrate the Eighteenth Sunday in Ordinary Time.

On this day, we hear the very interesting story of how God showered manna from heaven upon the Israelites in the desert. God had just rescued the Israelites from Egyptian slavery, and God had Moses and Aaron lead them out of Egypt to journey to the Promised Land. But instead of being grateful for the wonderful thing God had done for them, they instead complained about their diet. They were not satisfied.

Like the Israelites of old, we often find ourselves ungrateful for what we have. Rather than develop an attitude of gratitude, we develop an attitude of greed and ingratitude. We're never satisfied. We want more or different things.

But gratitude is a very important virtue in our spiritual life. It helps us cope with the ugliness of our world in beautiful ways. Take, for example, Matthew Henry. Henry was an English Protestant clergyman who lived from 1662-1714. Though he is best known for his Biblical commentaries, he was also noted for his attitude of gratitude.

One day, for example, while he was walking down the street, Henry was robbed. The thieves took everything of value that he had on him. Later that evening, he wrote the following in his diary:

> "I am thankful that during these years I have never been robbed until now. Also, even though they took my money, they did not take my life. And although they took all I had, it was not much. Finally, I am grateful that it was I who was robbed, not I who robbed."

What an incredible example of an "attitude of gratitude" this gentleman displayed in his diary entry. He was able to make this entry because he was predisposed toward gratitude. In other words, he trained himself to always look on the bright side of life and focus on the blessings inherent in challenges.

Unfortunately, though, we have many examples of how people have the very opposite of an attitude of gratitude. Their primary focus is on what they don't have. And it is good to explore their way of reacting to the world so that we may watch for seeds of such negativity

166

in our own spirits. Let me share an example from television, a show called "Bridezillas."

Though I am not a regular fan of this show, I have watched it a couple of times in utter amazement.

The typical bridezilla is a young woman who is preparing for her wedding. Her dream of one day getting married, which she has probably had ever since she first heard the story of Cinderella and her handsome young prince as a little girl, is about to come true. But instead of focusing on the joy of a dream come true, she throws temper tantrums over the tiniest things. Her phony eyelashes are not on straight. Her bridesmaids are not attentive enough to her. The caterer is two minutes late. The decorations are not up to her standards. Her dress is not exactly perfect. The hairdresser has not created the perfect hairdo. And the list goes on.

As I said, I watch in amazement. Here is this woman living in America, the land of opportunity. She has youth and a whole life ahead of her. She has a prince whom she is about to marry. She has eyes with which to see God's magnificent world, ears to hear beautiful music, senses to feel gentle breezes, hands to perform work and to feed herself, and legs to walk. Instead of focusing on what she has, she flies into ugly rages and is mean to anyone who comes into her path.

As I watch the program, I say to myself, "Well, this has to be fiction. It couldn't possibly be reality. Nobody could be that spoiled or mean or shallow." And I can just imagine, as I say these words, people in the congregation are smiling and saying to themselves, "WANNA BET?"

Although I say further to myself, "Certainly there could not be a man in America stupid enough to marry such a mean creature," the final scene always shows a smiling bride and groom standing in front of the preacher pledging their love for each other.

Does an "attitude of gratitude" mean that we are never to be sad or angry or disappointed? Of course not. Rather, an "attitude of gratitude" means that we are so focused on the gifts that God gives us, that when bad things happen to us, or when we don't get what we want, our natural inclination is to focus on what we do have, rather on what we don't, and even to look for a blessing hidden in the deprivation.

As we continue our life journeys this week, it would be a good idea to take some time to examine our own lives. Are we persons with an "attitude of gratitude?" Or are we more like the infamous Bridezillas of television?

And that is the good news I have for you on this Eighteenth Sunday in Ordinary Time.

Story source: Matthew Henry's journal note, "Gratitude," in Raymond McHenry (Ed.), *Something to Think About*, 1998, p. 118.

Chapter 42

19th Sunday in Ordinary Time – B

Eucharist as Healing

Scripture:

- 1 Kings 19: 4-8
- Psalm 34: 2-3, 4-5, 6-7, 8-9
- Ephesians 4: 30 – 5: 2
- John 6: 41-51

Today Catholic Christians celebrate the Nineteenth Sunday in Ordinary Time.

In the last few weeks, we have been hearing stories from the Old and New Testaments that are often called "Eucharistic stories." We have learned several things about the Eucharist. For example, we learned that it is a gift from God. We learned that when God takes ordinary things such as manna in the desert or bread and wine and blesses them, they are sufficient to fill us. We learned that the Eucharist is something we are to share with others. We learned that when we come to Eucharist, we are to be changed into better people.

Today we encounter more Eucharistic stories, and today we learn that not only is Eucharistic food sufficient for filling us up, it is also good for healing.

One person who found out in a very dramatic way about the healing nature of Communion was St. Catherine of Genoa, who lived from 1447-1510.

Though she wanted to become a nun from the time she was thirteen years old, the convent told her she was too young. Then, when she was sixteen years old, her family forced her to marry a man named Giuliano. This politically-arranged marriage was a mismatch from the very beginning. Catherine was a very intense and humorless woman who was not easy to live with. Giuliano was a hot-tempered, pleasure-loving man who was frequently unfaithful to her.

Because of Giuliano's wild lifestyle, the couple faced financial ruin. After ten years of marriage, Catherine decided she couldn't take it any longer. So she prayed that God would make her sick enough to stay in bed for months.

But God did not answer her prayers that way. Rather, he led Catherine to visit her sister who was a nun at a local convent. There, Catherine asked for her sister's blessing. After the blessing, Catherine was so overcome by God's love, that she made a general Confession and then received Holy Communion for the first time in many years. And from that time on, she became a daily communicant, which was very unusual for lay people in those days.

Catherine's prayers eventually converted her husband, whereupon they moved to a poor section of Genoa and lived as brother and sister.

170

They devoted themselves to caring for the sick in this area. After some time, Catherine and Giuliano moved into the hospital to care for the sick with greater intensity. Catherine proved to be a remarkably competent nurse and hospital administrator, especially in 1493 when eighty percent of the city of Genoa died from the plague.

From the story of St. Catherine, we learn how powerful the Eucharist is for its healing nature. This is a supremely important point.

We see the foreshadowing of this principle in today's Old Testament story of Elijah the prophet. Elijah, the most outstanding prophet of the Old Testament and often called the "grandest and most romantic" character that Israel ever produced, one day became totally disgusted with himself. His energy was drained, and his zest for life and ministry had come to an end.

Disgusted with himself, Elijah sat down under a broom tree and told God to take him. But instead of granting Elijah death, God gave him a hearth cake and a jug of water to give him renewed energy and hope. After eating the bread and drinking the water, Elijah embarked on a journey of forty days and forty nights to Horeb, the mountain of God.

This story is a foreshadowing of the Eucharist. Elijah's depression symbolizes our own illnesses and weaknesses. The hearth cake and water are a foreshadowing of the bread and wine that Jesus would take and turn into His Body and Blood. The journey of forty days and forty nights is symbolic of our own vocation, our own walk to Lord. The fact that Elijah was transformed from a man praying for death into a man with the energy and determination to walk successfully through life to the Lord, shows us the healing nature of the Eucharist. And in the Gospel reading, Jesus indeed does say that the bread he would give would be life-giving.

In the seminary, we were taught that the Eucharist or Mass is the primary sacrament of forgiveness. It helps make us whole, strong, and holy. But it is also a powerful sacrament of healing. Perhaps this is why priests often tell boys and girls a message like this on their First Communion day: "No matter where your life takes you, always stay close to Jesus in the Blessed Sacrament. Come to love Communion and receive it often. And no matter what will happen to you in your life, Jesus will give you special graces that come from the Eucharist."

Unfortunately, we often forget this advice. So today, let's make a renewed effort to receive Jesus in the Blessed Sacrament as he commanded us over two thousand years ago and which the Church advises us today.

And that is the good news I have for you on this Nineteenth Sunday in Ordinary Time.

Story source: "St. Catherine of Genoa," in Sarah Fawcett Thomas (Revision Editor), *Butler's Lives of the Saints, New Full Edition – September*, Collegeville, MN, Burns & Oates/The Liturgical Press, 2000, pp. 131-135.

Chapter 43

20th Sunday in Ordinary Time – B

Wisdom and the Eucharist

<u>Scripture:</u>

- Proverbs 9: 1-6
- Psalm 34: 2-3, 4-5, 6-7
- Ephesians 5: 15-20
- John 6: 51-58

Today Catholic Christians celebrate the Twentieth Sunday in Ordinary Time.

On this day, we encounter a beautiful image from the Book of Proverbs. In this passage, there are two principles, disguised as women, named Wisdom and Folly. Wisdom leads to a fullness of life, while Folly leads to death.

In today's passage the focus is on Wisdom, who is throwing a banquet. Everyone who comes to the banquet is asked to cast aside their foolishness so that they may advance in understanding. By eating at the table prepared by Lady Wisdom, the guests will have an abundance of life.

This selection is a foreshadowing of the Eucharist, tying in very well with today's Gospel passage in which Jesus tells us about the life-giving nature of the Bread of Life.

Before discussing wisdom and the benefits of eating the Body of Christ, let us look at a story of wisdom, a very important Christian virtue.

It was nighttime when a great Teacher and his disciples sat around a blazing fire. They talked about many different things, and sometimes they remained silent as they gazed at the stars or looked at the glowing embers of the fire. Suddenly, the Teacher asked this question: "How can we know when the night has ended and the day has begun?"

One of the young disciples eagerly answered, "You know the night is over when you can look off in the distance and tell which animal is a dog and which is a sheep. Is that the right answer, Teacher?"

"It is a good answer," the Teacher said slowly, "but it isn't quite the answer I would give."

A second disciple offered another answer, saying, "You know the night is over when the light falls on the leaves and you can tell whether it is an olive tree or a fig tree."

Again the Teacher said, "That was a fine answer, but it is not the answer I seek."

Immediately the students began to argue with one another. Finally, one of the young women said, "Teacher, please answer your own question, for we cannot think of another response."

The Teacher looked intently at the eager faces of his disciples before he spoke. Then he said, "When you look into the eyes of another

174

human being and see a brother or sister, you will know it is morning. If you cannot see a brother or sister, you will know that no matter what time it is, for you it will always be night and you will always be in the dark."

What a beautiful story this is, for it captures well the nature of wisdom. Wisdom is the quality of judging rightly and following the soundest course of action. Simply possessing knowledge does not guarantee being wise. We all know many highly educated people with lots of advanced degrees who don't follow sound courses of action in their lives. On the other hand, we all know very wise people who may not even know how to read and write, yet live lives filled with right decisions and abundance.

But why would the Church have this selection from Proverbs today? Why is this a foreshadowing of the Eucharist?

To answer this question, we need to look at what Jesus is telling us about the Eucharist. He tells us that

"...unless you eat the flesh of the Son of Man and drink his blood, you do not have life within you. Whoever eats my flesh and drinks my blood has eternal life..." (John 6: 53-54).

In other words, the Eucharist is supposed to produce some existential changes in us. We are not supposed to leave the church building on Sunday as the same person we were when we came in. We are intended to have grown. Furthermore, we are to show our growth in our actions. Just like the guests at Lady Wisdom's banquet, we too are to discard the old self and put on a new self. We are to grow in virtue, just as the wedding guests of Lady Wisdom's banquet table advanced in understanding.

Unfortunately, though, growth is usually a slow process. Virtues like prudence and wisdom tend to be found predominately in older folks. They obtain such virtues only through painful life experiences and mistakes they made along the way. For example, many of us who are wise in saving money and prudent in spending money have not always been that way. Many of us arrived at this only by frivolous spending and a mountain of credit card debt in our younger days.

As we continue our life journey this week, it might be a good idea to examine our lives. What kind of changes do we see from our participation in the Eucharist? How do we try to be better people as a result of Mass?

And that is the good news I have for you on this Twentieth Sunday in Ordinary Time.

Story source: Anonymous, "Night and Day," in Brian Cavanaugh (Ed.), *Fresh Packet of Seeds: Third Planting*, New York: Paulist Press, 1994, #65, pp. 61-62.

Chapter 44

21st Sunday in Ordinary Time – B

Arua

<u>Scripture:</u>

- Joshua 24: 1-2a, 15-17, 18b
- Psalm 34: 2-3, 16-17, 18-19, 20-21
- Ephesians 5: 21-32
- John 6: 60-69

Today Catholic Christians celebrate the Twenty-First Sunday in Ordinary Time.

On this day, we celebrate the Missionary Cooperation Plan at our parish. The Missionary Cooperation Plan, a project of the Society for the Propagation of the Faith, is international in scope. On one weekend each year, a missionary order or diocese comes to each parish to tell about life in his or her part of the world. We, as American Catholics, take up a collection to help in the international mission.

As the director of foreign missions for our diocese, I invite various orders or dioceses to our diocese and assign them to various parishes. This year I chose the Diocese of Arua in Uganda to visit us here in our parish. Unfortunately the diocese was unable to send a spokesperson. Fortunately, though, I am able to speak on their behalf, as I know this diocese from previous visits.

The Diocese of Arua is one of nineteen dioceses in Uganda. It is one of the poorest of the dioceses, and Uganda is one of the poorest countries in Africa. The diocese is in the West Nile Region, in the northwest corner of Uganda. The region borders Sudan and the Democratic Republic of Congo. It encompasses more than 4,000 square miles and has a population of more than 1,650,000, 41% of them being Catholic. There are approximately 7,600 Catholics per ordained priest; this compares to 1,200 Catholics per priest in the Diocese of Raleigh and 9,700 Catholics per priest in the Archdiocese of Tegucigalpa to which our sister parish belongs.

Life is very hard in this part of Uganda. For the most part, electricity has not yet come to the Diocese of Arua, and most people do not have running water. People spend much of their days walking to and from wells for water, or looking for firewood.

The diocese is almost entirely rural, and people try to make a living by farming. Unfortunately, the people lack basic farm tools, so they have to engage in the backbreaking work of plowing up the land with old hoes and planting seed by hand.

Health care is very primitive. Hospitals have what I would describe as pre-World War I supplies—if that. Schools are also very poor, and the only classroom some children have is the shade of a large tree.

In spite of all their difficulties, the people have great faith. Like Catholic Christians the world over, Ugandans live out their faith in a parish. The parishes, though, are vastly different from those in the United States. Their parishes have many churches and chapels, and the priest needs to travel on basically non-existent roads to get to the churches. Typical parishes have between 22,000 to 26,000 Catholics. Needless to say, the people get to celebrate Mass only once in a while. Priests usually travel on old motorcycles that frequently break down.

Many of the churches in the Diocese of Arua have grass roofs. Because there is no electricity, such churches are very dark inside. Because of the dryness of the grass roofs, the priests dare not use kerosene lanterns for fear that a spark might ignite the roofs and burn down the church. Therefore, the priests must memorize a great deal, as they can't see well in the dark spaces, and if they need glasses, they usually can't afford them.

I don't need to explain that poverty is the biggest problem in this country, and while there I met people who eat only every other day so that everyone in the family could have at least some food.

To complicate pastoral ministry even more is the fact that many different languages are spoken in Uganda. Although English is one of the official languages and is taught in the schools, it is generally not the principal language spoken at home. In one parish I visited, the congregation used fifty-two different languages. Ugandan priests, therefore, must celebrate Mass in many languages.

Unlike American parishes that usually only have one church facility and perhaps a school, convent, and rectory, Ugandan parishes have a variety of places of worship. In addition, it is not uncommon for parishes to have clinics, vocational training centers, outdoor kitchens to feed the workers, farm animals, woodworking shops, catechist-training houses, etc.

Celebrating Mass on Sundays in Uganda tends to be very joyful, very lively, and very long. There is much liturgical dancing and vibrant music with primitive instruments and drums. One of the sounds at liturgy completely foreign to Americans is called "ululation," a very high-pitched, eerie piercing sound made by women. It would be very hard to fall asleep at a Ugandan Mass!

You and I have been blessed beyond the wildest dreams of the overwhelming majority of the world. That is the good news. The sobering news, though, is that Jesus reminded us that the more we have, the more will be expected of us in terms of generosity. Please be generous in giving to our less fortunate brothers and sisters of the world.

And that is the good news I have for you on this Twenty-First Sunday in Ordinary Time.

Chapter 45

22nd Sunday in Ordinary Time – B

Sr. Ignatia of A.A.

Scripture:

- Deuteronomy 4: 1-2, 6-8
- Psalm 15: 2-3a, 3bc-4ab, 5
- James 1: 17-18, 21b-22, 27
- Mark 7: 1-8, 14-15, 21-23

Today Catholic Christians celebrate the Twenty-Second Sunday in Ordinary time.

In today's Gospel reading from St. Mark, certain Pharisees and Scribes complained to Jesus that they had observed his disciples violating the cleanliness codes of the Jewish people. Specifically, they complained that Jesus' disciples did not wash their hands before eating.

Jesus answered the Scribes and Pharisees by saying, "You disregard God's commandment but cling to human tradition." In other words, they were so enamored by human-made rules, that they put the rules ahead of God's commandment to love.

Humanity has always struggled with the tendency to forget that laws and rules and customs are to serve humanity, to help us maintain order for a smooth life. They are not to be worshiped as the Scribes and Pharisees were doing. One Catholic American hero who understood that love always prevails was Sr. Ignatia of Ohio.

Sr. Ignatia was a member of the Sisters of Charity of St. Augustine, the religious order who taught me in elementary school. Sr. Ignatia taught music for twenty-one years, but at the age of 39, while recovering from a nervous breakdown, she was assigned to be the registration clerk at St. Thomas Hospital in Akron, Ohio, birthplace of Alcoholics Anonymous.

In the summer of 1939, a physician named Bob Smith, co-founder of Alcoholics Anonymous, came to Sr. Ignatia. He wanted to have a detoxification center in the hospital where alcoholics could get medical supervision while sobering up, and then learn a new way of life. Sr. Ignatia was all for the idea, for like Dr. Bob, she knew what suffering and compassionate treatment were all about.

The hospital administration, however, was quite against the idea. They told Dr. Bob, himself a recovering alcoholic, that they did not want alcoholics at St. Thomas Hospital. Sr. Ignatia and Dr. Bob ignored the administration, and they cooked up different ideas to get alcoholics admitted. Sr. Ignatia would, for example, admit alcoholic patients during shift changes while nursing supervisors were busy with reports. Or the alcoholic patients would be admitted under different diagnoses such as gastritis.

182

Eventually, though, Dr. Bob and Sr. Ignatia had to confront the issue in the open. Due to their firm stance, the hospital administrator, Sr. Clementine, agreed to open the first alcoholic unit, which used the spiritual program of Alcoholics Anonymous as its basic treatment strategy. Between 1939 and 1950, more than five thousand alcoholics were treated at St. Thomas Hospital.

Then in 1952, at age 63, Sr. Ignatia was transferred to St. Vincent Charity Hospital in Cleveland, Ohio. Immediately she began making plans for the hospital to build a new alcoholism treatment center, which she named Rosary Hall Solarium, a ward that had the same initials as Dr. Bob—Robert Holbrook Smith.

Just as in Akron, Sr. Ignatia had to fight for what she wanted. In the book "Sister Ignatia: Angel of Alcoholics Anonymous" author Mary Darrah wrote of one incident showing Sr. Ignatia's spirit:

> "As part of the ward's setup, [Sr. Ignatia] requested a coffee bar for the patients, similar to the one in Akron. However, a board member who reviewed the plan questioned the need for it. He returned the plan to Sr. Ignatia and said, 'A table will have to do.' But Ignatia would not compromise. She knew what she wanted for the AAs, and she put the future of the ward on the line with her reply: 'Let's forget about it if you're not going to give us the proper setup.' The coffee bar remained in the drawings."

Sr. Ignatia got her way by putting love above law, compassion above rules. And to the alcoholics who were served at Rosary Hall she gave a badge of the Sacred Heart of Jesus. The people who accepted the badge promised to return the badge to her before taking another drink of alcohol. This custom survives down to this day in the form of tokens marking anniversaries of sobriety in AA.

The life of Sr. Ignatia reminds us that love should always prevail over laws and rules and customs, and that for faith to fully be alive, it must be put into action.

And that is the good news I have for you on this Twenty-Second Sunday in Ordinary Time.

Story source: Mary C. Darrah, *Sister Ignatia: Angel of Alcoholics Anonymous,* Chicago: Loyola University Press, 1992.

Chapter 46

23rd Sunday in Ordinary Time – B

Pastor and Shoemaker

<u>Scripture:</u>

- Isaiah 35: 4-7a
- Psalm 146: 6c-7, 8-9a, 9bc-10
- James 2: 1-5
- Mark 7: 31-37

Today Catholic Christians celebrate the Twenty-Third Sunday in Ordinary Time.

In today's New Testament reading, St. James tells us that as Christian people, we should never show partiality. In other words, we should treat all people equally.

The early Christians to whom James wrote were often treating rich people better than poor people. They would give seats to the rich while making the poor stand. James, of course, condemned this behavior.

As Christians, we sometimes forget that in the eyes of God, each person is special. Each person is a child of God. Though we profess this belief, we don't always put it into practice. That is what happened to a priest in the following story.

There was once a priest who had just received his first pastoral assignment. As a new pastor, he was filled with enthusiasm for his new parish and wanted to do a great job. So, one day he took a walk around the streets of his new parish to meet the people. One of his first stops was at the local shoemaker's shop.

The priest talked with the shoemaker using, at times, some very lofty theological language. The priest was very surprised that not only did the shoemaker understand what he was saying, but also replied with keen understanding and some deep spiritual insights. The priest was very surprised and said, "You shouldn't be cobbling shoes. A man with your understanding and clear manner of expressing those thoughts should not be doing such menial and secular work."

The shoemaker became very angry at the words of the priest and said, "Father, take that back right now!"

The priest, very surprised, said, "Take what back?"

"Take back," the shoemaker replied, "that I'm just doing menial, secular work." The shoemaker continued. "Do you see that pair of boots on the shelf? They belong to the son of the Widow Smith, whose husband died last year. The only support she has is from her son, who works outdoors every day. I have heard that some bad weather is coming into the area, and I felt the Lord saying to me, 'Will you make Widow Smith's son some shoes so he won't catch cold and come down with some sickness?' I replied, 'Certainly, Lord, I will.'"

186

Looking at the priest, the shoemaker said, "Father, I trust that you preach your homilies under God's direction. I make and fix shoes under God's direction. One day, when we both get to heaven and the final rewards are given out, I expect to hear the Harvest Master say to you and me both, in the same way, 'Well done, my good and faithful servant.'"

In this story, the humble shoemaker gives the ordained priest an important lesson: all people should be treated with dignity and respect.

Sometimes we forget this principle just as the people in the early Church were forgetting it by treating the rich better than the poor among them. We fancy that some people are superior to others and should be treated as superior. This is not in harmony with what James is trying to teach us, and certainly not in harmony with Jesus' continual emphasis on how leaders must be servants. Sometimes, we need to be challenged. We need to be forced to confront our views of human dignity. Do we really believe all people are equal? Certainly Catholics, and Americans in general, claim they believe that. But in the deepest parts of our hearts, do we really?

Here is a little "quiz" that I put together in honor of the Silver Rose program that our Knights of Columbus held recently, in honor of respecting human beings. I ask you to thoughtfully consider your answers: Do you believe that:

- the life of a man is equal to the life of a woman;
- the life of an Iraqi or Mexican is equal to the life of an American;
- the life of a single person is equal to the life of a married person;
- the life of a person with children is equal to the life of a person without children;
- the life of a prisoner is equal to the life of a free person;
- the life of a born person is equal to the life of an unborn person;
- the life of a soldier is equal to the life of a civilian;
- the life of a brown or black skinned person is equal to the life of a white person;
- the life of an atheist is equal to the life of a Catholic Christian;
- the life of a gay or lesbian person is equal to the life of a heterosexual;

- the life of a homeless person is equal to the life of a person with a home;
- the life of a poor person is equal to the life of a rich person;
- the life of an older person is equal to the life of a young person?

Obviously, the list could go on and on. As Catholic Christians, our answers should solidly be "Yes!" to each and every question. Did the quiz make you uncomfortable? Do you believe "deep down" that some people should be treated with greater respect than others? Or did you wholeheartedly answer "yes" to each question?

And that is the good news I have for you on this Twenty-Third Sunday in Ordinary Time.

Story source: Anonymous, "The Pastor and the Cobbler," in Brian Cavanaugh (Ed.),*Sower's Seeds that Nurture Family Values: Sixth Printing,* New York: Paulist Press, 2000, #35, pp. 44-45.

Chapter 47

24th Sunday in Ordinary Time – B

The Shaving Master

Scripture:

- Isaiah 50: 5-9a
- Psalm 116: 1-2, 3-4, 5-6, 8-9
- James 2: 14-18
- Mark 8: 27-35

Today Catholic Christians celebrate the Twenty-Fourth Sunday in Ordinary Time.

On this day, we read from one of my very favorite parts of the Bible, the Letter of James. This New Testament book is a very clear and practical document that teaches Christians how to put their Faith into practice. It beautifully reflects the basic principles of Catholic social teaching.

In today's selection, St. James reminds the early Christians that faith without works is basically meaningless. He says:

> "If a brother or sister has nothing to wear and has no food for the day, and one of you says to them, 'Go in peace, keep warm, and eat well,' but you do not give them the necessities of the body, what good is it? So also faith of itself, if it does not have works, is dead" (James 2: 15-17).

Sometimes people mistakenly think that putting Faith into action necessarily involves doing great, heroic things. However, most of the ways we put faith into action involve very basic and simple things. That is what we see in the following story.

Every evening between 6 and 7 p.m. the manager of a feed mill in Edgerton, Wisconsin packs a little bag and walks to a nearby local hospital. When he gets inside, he goes down the hallways looking into patient rooms. To each man he encounters he asks, "Would you like a shave tonight?"

Usually the patients are surprised, for this visitor is often a stranger to them. But if they say that they would like a shave, the feed mill manager comes in, opens his bag, removes an electric shaver, and gives them a clean shave while cheerily chatting with them. He is usually gone before the patients can even thank him.

The volunteer barber's name is Norman, and over the years, he has visited the hospital every night and has shaved over thirty thousand patients. It all began one day when his father-in-law, a patient at the hospital, asked Norman if he would come to the hospital and shave him. Norman brought his old-style razor, soap and brush and went to work.

He did it so well that his father-in-law's roommate asked for a shave also. Soon, news of this "shaving master" began to spread throughout the entire hospital. Soon, Norman changed to an electric shaver to serve more patients more quickly.

The hospital staff loved Norman's service, and patients felt so much better after being shaved. Norman found that giving himself to others in this simple way brought him a deep and joyful satisfaction.

Norman, a husband and father, is active in his local church and has served as an alderman and a volunteer firefighter in his community.

A minister who once benefited from Norman's free shave said, "Shaving a man seems like a simple act, yet it is Christianity at work—a man doing something to show his love for his brother."

Many people think that Catholic Christians do good works because they suppose that by doing so, they are "earning" salvation. This is, of course, a falsehood. Nobody can "earn" heaven, for this is a gift. We do good works because of Jesus Christ. He said that we are to serve him by serving our brothers and sisters in need. He said that when we serve others, we actually are serving Him, for He lives in each of us.

Opportunities to serve others are limitless. In our own parish community, for example, we put our Faith into action in more than seventy major ministries and several minor ones. For example, we serve others as:

- Camillus Ministers, bringing Holy Communion to our community's biggest hospital and hospice, fifteen nursing homes, and many private homes;
- CARE Ministers, bringing hope and joy to those affected by HIV and AIDS;
- Teachers and catechists, bringing knowledge and values to students in the schools of our parish;
- Hispanic Ministers, bringing the Faith to the Catholic immigrants who bring such joy and rich diversity to our parish life;
- Carpenters, plumbers, electricians, and others, who bring needed construction to meet our basic needs;
- Missionaries, bringing an American Catholic presence to the mountains of Honduras;

- Landscapers, bringing beauty to our surroundings;
- Music ministers, enriching our worship with song;
- Dentists and oral surgeons, serving the poor in our St. Mary Health Center;
- Volunteers, serving thousands of poor people in our outreach ministry;
- and many, many others.

Putting our Faith into action is easy, and the opportunities to do so are limitless. How do you put your Faith into action?

And that is the good news I have for you on this Twenty-Fourth Sunday in Ordinary Time.

Story source: "The Shaving Master," in *Friends in Deed: Stories about Acts of Kindness: A Guidepost Book*, Nashville, TN: Dimensions for Living, 1997, pp. 168-169.

Chapter 48

25th Sunday in Ordinary Time – B

San Juan Macías

<u>Scripture:</u>

- Wisdom 2: 12, 17-20
- Psalm 54: 3-4, 5, 6 & 8
- James 3: 16 – 4: 3
- Mark 9: 30-37

Today Catholic Christians celebrate the Twenty-Fifth Sunday in Ordinary Time.

On this day, also known as Catechetical Sunday, we encounter a beautiful reading from St. James. In this reading, James reminds us that jealousy and selfish ambition can only lead to disorder and "every foul practice." When we are not selfish, though, we are filled with mercy and good fruits, and these lead us to a peaceful existence.

A wonderful model of an unselfish person was St. Juan Macías who lived from 1585 to 1645.

Born in Spain, Juan became an orphan when he was only four years old. His uncle then took him into his household and trained him to be a shepherd. Juan loved being a shepherd because it gave him a lot of time to pray and meditate.

When he was a young man, however, Juan had a vision telling him that he should leave Spain and go to the New World, where many of his countrymen were spreading the good news of Jesus Christ as Catholic Christian missionaries.

Thanks to a wealthy businessman, Juan was able to make his dream a reality. He first worked around Cartagena, Colombia, and then Quito, Ecuador. When he was thirty-five, he went to Lima, Peru, where he gave away all he had to the poor.

After a couple of years working on a ranch near Lima, he entered the Dominican Friary as a Brother. In 1623, when he was thirty-eight, he took his final vows.

In the friary, Juan was assigned to be the porter or doorkeeper. This job he did only out of obedience, because it did not suit his personal preferences. If it had been up to him, he would rather have served completely behind the scenes, never interacting with the public.

As the porter, Juan came into contact with all kinds of people from the streets of Lima. He was especially devoted to and loved by the poor, the sick, the disabled, and the suffering. His sensitivity and compassion for them knew no limits. This devotion came, in large part, from his own background of poverty and abandonment.

As the porter, it was also his job to beg for food, medicines and money for the poor and sick of the community. He even trained a donkey to go through the city with baskets on its back for people to put in food, medicines, and money. The donkey, after making its rounds, would come back to Brother Juan.

Though his first love was the poor and marginalized, he was also a friend to the rich of Lima, who recognized his great holiness. They too came to the friary to seek his counsel.

Even though Brother Juan would have much preferred to live in solitude, he faithfully carried out his duties as porter of the friary. During his lifetime, the people of Lima attributed many miracles to him, including multiplication of rice for a poor community.

Brother Juan, friend of St. Martin de Porres, died in 1645 and was canonized in 1975.

St. Juan Macías is a model for us today in many ways. First, he lived his life free of the "selfish ambitions" that St. James condemned in today's Scripture. And because he lived his life in that way, he was able to be "other-directed" instead of "inner-directed." That means that he was able to touch the minds and hearts of people of all races and classes of his society. That, in St. James' language, is the "fruit" of his life.

Second, St. Juan shows us that we can live our vocations in excellent ways even when we hold jobs that might be contrary to our basic nature. Though St. Juan would much have preferred to be more of a hermit, he was able to live out his life as a porter in an excellent way.

Third, he shows us how important suffering can be in developing sensitivity and compassion. This is exactly what the twentieth-century Catholic spiritual writer, Fr. Henri Nouwen, meant by the term "wounded healer." Only when one suffers can one understand suffering, and only when one is part of the community of those who suffer can one totally identify with their challenges and triumphs.

Finally, St. Juan Macías is a wonderful example for catechists on this Catechetical Sunday. Catechists, as we know, are commissioned to spread the Catholic Christian Faith. Usually when we think of their role, we think of them as teachers in a classroom. However, when we try to encourage virtues in others, it is much more effective to model the virtues than merely to talk about them. This is what is called being "living homilies." All catechists are called to be living homilies, with St. Juan as an example.

As we continue our life journeys this week, it would be a good idea to ask ourselves: How is "selfish ambition" present in my life? How can I root out this spiritual weed so I can produce good fruit?

And that is the good news I have for you on this Twenty-Fifth Sunday in Ordinary Time.

Story sources:
- "St. John Macías," in Sarah Fawcett Thomas (Revision Editor), *Butler's Lives of the Saints: Full Edition – September*, Collegeville, MN: Burns & Oates/The Liturgical Press, 2000, p. 154.
- Fr. Robert J. Kus, "St. Juan Macías," in *Saintly Men of Nursing: 100 Amazing Stories*, Wilmington, N.C.: Red Lantern Press, 2017, 163-164.

Chapter 49

26th Sunday in Ordinary Time – B

Fr. Mychal Judge

<u>Scripture:</u>

- Numbers 11: 25-29
- Psalm 19: 8, 10, 12-13, 14
- James 5: 1-6
- Mark 9: 38-43, 45, 47-48

Today Catholic Christians celebrate the Twenty-Sixth Sunday in Ordinary Time, and once again, we hear from St. James. In today's selection, we hear about the folly of material wealth, for when we die, we will not be able to take the things of the world with us. Rather, we should set our sites on eternal values rather than on fleeting earthly things.

One American Catholic hero who turned his back on the material world and gave his heart to eternal values was a Franciscan priest named Mychal Judge.

Robert Emmet Judge, who took the name of Mychal when he entered the Franciscan order, was born in 1933 in Brooklyn, the son of Irish Catholic immigrants. There he grew up with his twin sister and their older sister during the Great Depression. From a very early age, he was attracted to the poor, and he was known to give away his only coin to beggars.

When he was just six years old, Robert went to work in Penn Station, shining shoes to help his family. His father, dying from cancer, could not work. After working, Robert would go to a nearby church named St. Francis of Assisi where he met the Franciscan friars. From a very early age, he knew that he did not care about material things and that one day, he too would be a friar.

When he was fifteen years old, Robert began his formation process to become a Franciscan priest and took the name of Mychal. He was ordained in 1961.

As a Franciscan, he served in Boston, New Jersey, and New York State until he finally was assigned to the monastery of St. Francis of Assisi on West 31st Street in New York City. There he lived until his death in 2001.

As a priest, Mychal was known for his great compassion and sensitivity, much of it gained because he was a "wounded healer." In particular, as a recovering alcoholic, he was able to be an especially powerful blessing to alcoholics and those suffering from other illnesses.

Fr. Mychal was known for his ministry to the homeless, the hungry, people with AIDS, the sick, the injured, the grieving, immigrants, and those who had been alienated by religious leaders.

As with St. Teresa of Calcutta, there are many stories about Fr. Mychal and his compassion. One day, for example, after he anointed a man dying from AIDS, the man asked Fr. Mychal if he thought that God hated him. Fr. Mychal picked the man up, kissed him, and rocked him silently in his arms. Likewise, it was not at all uncommon for Fr. Mychal to give the coat off his back to a person who was cold and had no coat.

In prayer Mychal would sometimes become so deeply immersed that he would go into a trance-like state and be shocked afterward to learn that several hours had passed. As one of his spiritual directors said after Fr. Mychal's death, "We knew we were dealing with someone directly in line with God."

But of all Mychal's ministries, his favorite was being Chaplain to the Fire Department of New York. There was nothing he would not do for the men and women of the Department, and he often worked sixteen-hour days on their behalf. Just as he loved the Department, the members of the Department deeply loved him.

On September 11, 2001, Fr. Mychal heard the news that shook the world: terrorists had flown airliners into the World Trade Center. Without wasting a minute, Fr. Mychal rushed to the scene, where Mayor Giuliani met him. Fr. Mychal anointed people lying in the streets and gave whatever comfort he could. Fr. Mychal went inside the north tower lobby, and was killed by flying debris. A photographer took a photo of Fr. Mychal's body being carried out by five men, and a Philadelphia newspaper called the photo "an American *Pieta*."

Fr. Mychal's body bag was tagged "Victim 0001," the very first person known to have lost his life in the terrorist attack.

After his death, Fr. Mychal's helmet was presented to Pope John Paul II, and France awarded him the *Légion d'honneur*. The US Congress nominated him for a Presidential Medal of Freedom, New York City renamed a part of West 31st Street "Father Mychal F. Judge Street," and many buildings and ships have been named after him.

Catholic Christians throughout the world, especially in the United States, pray for his canonization.

Fr. Mychal Judge is a genuine American Catholic hero. He never allowed himself to fall in love with the material world. He never allowed possessions to possess him. Rather, he gave his heart and soul to brave men and women who put their lives on the line for us, and to other men and women who had been battered by life in many ways.

As we continue our life journeys this week, it would be a good idea to ask ourselves this question: How do I show that I own my possessions and that my possessions do not own me?

And that is the good news I have for you on this Twenty-Sixth Sunday in Ordinary Time.

Story source: Ford, Michael, *Father Mychal Judge: An Authentic American Hero*, Mahwah, N.J.: Paulist Press, 2002.

Chapter 50

27th Sunday in Ordinary Time – B

Witness of Faith

<u>Scripture:</u>

- Genesis 2: 18-24
- Psalm 128: 1-2, 3, 4-5, 6
- Hebrews 2: 9-11
- Mark 10: 2-16

Today the Church celebrates the Twenty-Seventh Sunday in Ordinary Time, also called Respect Life Sunday.

At first glance, it seems strange that the primary theme of the Scripture readings is that of marriage and divorce. But on second thought, it makes sense. After all, it is in part through our vocations, including marriage and family, that we gain the fullness of life—our mental, physical, and spiritual health.

In the following story, we see how a teenager brought new life to a man whose marriage was in trouble.

There was once a teenager named Anne who got a summer job in housekeeping in an oceanside hotel. Each day, she had to clean ten rooms. During the course of the summer, she met all kinds of interesting people, including a few celebrities. The person who stood out from all the others, though, was Mr. Smith.

Mr. Smith came to the hotel one weekend with only an overnight bag. When Anne went to clean his room, he stuck his head out the door and said, "Forget about cleaning my room. Just give me clean towels." The next couple of days he did exactly the same. Only until mid-week did Mr. Smith allow Anne to clean his room. As she cleaned, he talked with her and even helped her make the bed.

On Saturday, after Anne cleaned her ten rooms, she began walking down the lane to 4:30 p.m. Mass. Suddenly, Mr. Smith's car pulled up next to her and asked if he could give her a ride. She readily agreed.

Once inside the car, Mr. Smith asked Anne lots of questions such as how often she went to Mass, how were the homilies, did she always receive Communion, and others. Anne replied, "Come and see."

When they got to church, Mr. Smith asked if he could go to Mass with her. She felt a little wary about this stranger and his questions, but she agreed. All through Mass, Mr. Smith was very reverent and seemed lost in prayer.

After Mass, Mr. Smith got up and hurried outside without even saying goodbye. The next day, when Anne went to clean his room, she discovered that Mr. Smith and his overnight bag were gone. In its place was a small box with a note that read:

"Dear Anne,

The gift inside the box is for the beautiful thing you've done for me without even knowing it. My marriage has been rather shaky lately—so much so that I finally told my wife that I was moving out for a few days to think things over. The more I thought, the more confused I got.

Then you came along. You invited me to 'come and see.' Your beautiful faith in God touched me deeply. When I attended Mass with you, it was for the first time in ten years. During that Mass God gave me an insight into my problems and the desire to stay with my wife.

I'm going home, grateful to God and grateful to you for being a shining light in a time when my world was very dark. I will never forget you for helping me rediscover my faith. [Signed] Mr. Smith."

Inside the box was a gold chain with a beautiful gold cross attached to it.

Though this beautiful story had a romantic ending, not all marriage stories are "happily ever after." Some are not happy and some do end in divorce. From my experience as a priest who counsels people with divorce experience, here are three points to ponder.

First, not all marriages are sacramental in nature. In other words, many marriages have some flaw in them from the very beginning. Sometimes these flaws do not show up until years into the marriage. The Church often declares such marriages "null."

Second, don't judge people because of divorce. You have not walked in their shoes, and you don't know what has occurred behind closed doors. Sometimes people present themselves to the outside world as magnificent human beings, but with their spouse and children, they may be very different. Oftentimes, spouses find that their marriage is destroying their own lives; they cannot grow spiritually, mentally, or physically in such an environment. Thus, they find themselves leaving in order to thrive.

Third, if you yourself have had a divorce and are unsure of your status in the Church community, please see me. I can't tell you how many go around with false information in their heads about divorce, receiving Communion, the nullity process, and the like. Don't be like the person who receives their religious information from a friend of a hairdresser who has a boyfriend who once lived next door to a woman who had a cousin who was a Catholic who said "x, y, or z" about the Church and its marriage teachings. Go to the priest who either has the correct information or who will get it for you.

And that is the good news I have for you on this Twenty-Seventh Sunday in Ordinary Time.

Story source: Anonymous, "Witness of Faith," in Brian Cavanaugh (Ed.), *Sower's Seeds Aplenty: Fourth Planting*, New York: Paulist Press, 1996, #27, pp. 20-21.

Chapter 51

28th Sunday in Ordinary Time – B

The Giving Tree

Scripture:

- Wisdom 7: 7-11
- Psalm 90: 12-13, 14-15, 16-17
- Hebrews 4: 12-13
- Mark 10: 17-30

Today Catholic Christians celebrate the Twenty-Eighth Sunday in Ordinary time.

On this day, we hear the sad story of a Jesus calling a young man to follow him. But first he asked the man to sell all he had and give it to the poor. Unfortunately, the young man had many possessions and could not stand to part with them. His possessions owned him, rather than him owning the possessions.

Though this story has a disheartening ending, it is a good one for us to hear, because it forces us to examine our own lives and ask ourselves some important questions such as: How do I handle the gifts of my life? How grateful am I for them? How generous am I? In other words, what kind of a steward am I?

Before exploring stewardship, though, let's examine the fascinating story of the giving tree.

There was once a very unusual and ancient tree that grew outside the gates of a desert city. In fact, the tree was so old that it was considered a landmark. This tree seemed to have been touched by the finger of God because it bore fruit perpetually. Despite its old age, the branches of the tree were always filled with delicious fruit. Hundreds of passersby helped themselves to the fruit of the tree, and it never failed to give freely of its fruit.

One day, however, a greedy merchant bought the property on which the tree grew. He jealously watched as hundreds of travelers picked the fruit from "his" tree. So he built a high fence around the tree so that nobody could get to the fruit. Desert travelers begged and begged him to share the fruit with them. The miserly merchant just replied, "It's my tree, my fruit, and I bought it with my own money. I won't share it with you."

In a short while, though, something amazing happened: suddenly, after giving its fruit to one and all for centuries, the ancient tree died! It died because the law of giving is as firm as the law of gravity: when giving stops, bearing fruit ceases, and death is certain to follow.

Like the giving tree, we too are called to be good stewards if we are to be spiritually alive. But what is a good steward?

Stewardship involves our time, talent, and treasure, and it has four parts. First, we are called to remember that all good gifts come from God. Therefore, we should be thankful for what we have and not focus on what we don't have.

Second, we are to develop our gifts to the best of our ability. We are not to be like the steward who buried his talent in the ground. In our society, one of the major ways of developing our gifts is through education.

Third, we are to share our gifts abundantly with those who could use them. There is no such thing as a "private gift" to be hoarded. Rather, every gift we have is social in nature. Catholic Christians are called especially to share what they have with those who have much less.

Finally, we are called to return to the Lord the first fruits of our labor. In American society, the "fruits of our labor" usually refers to money. "First fruits" refers to giving to the Lord "off the top." For example, as a person who is only paid once a month, my first check is to the Lord via my parish, and then I live on the rest.

Though stewardship involves time and talent as well as treasure, today I want to talk about the treasure aspect in this time of harvest.

Many times in the Bible, we hear about the call of the Lord to "tithe." Tithing means giving ten percent (10%) of one's income to the Lord. Catholic Christians often fall woefully short. I remember a young man from another parish telling me one day, "You know, Fr. Bob, I was driving down the street the other day and a terrible thought came into my head: I give more to my car each month than I give to the Lord!" The young man corrected this and began to be a faithful tithing person. Though he had a good job but not one that paid a huge amount, he was able to pay his mortgage off in three years from when he obtained it. Needless to say, I put him on our Finance Council! Today, he serves our diocese as a permanent deacon.

What would tithing look like if you gave 10% of your income to the Lord? Let's pretend that you live at the poverty level in the United States. Suppose you were to give 10% of your income to the Lord each week. If you are a single person, your tithe would be $22.85 per week. A couple would tithe $31.15 per week. And if you had a family of four, your tithe would be $46.73 per week. That is assuming, of course, that you are living at the 2016 poverty level.

Finally, remember that I will never ask you for an amount that I won't match double or triple, and my offer always stands that if God fails to bless you sufficiently because of your generosity, please come and see me and I'll try to get your offerings back to you.

And that is the good news I have for you on this Twenty-Eighth Sunday in Ordinary Time.

Story source: Anonymous, "A Giving Tree," in Brian Cavanaugh's *Sower's Seeds of Encouragement: Fifth Planting*, New York: Paulist Press, 1998, #62, p. 59.

Chapter 52

29ᵗʰ Sunday in Ordinary Time – B

Fr. Thomas Frederick Price

Scripture:

- Isaiah 53: 10-11
- Psalm 33: 4-5, 18-19, 20 & 22
- Hebrews 4: 14-16
- Mark 10: 35-45

Today Catholic Christians celebrate the Twenty-Ninth Sunday in Ordinary time. Also on this day, Catholic Christians throughout the world celebrate World Mission Sunday. Today, the pope asks all Catholic Christians to remember that our Church is universal: it has no boundaries. Following the command of Jesus, we are called to spread the Good News throughout the world. On this day, we specifically vow to support the missionaries who serve on the front lines of the world's mission territories with our prayers and our financial assistance.

In the early days of our country, our entire continent was considered a mission territory. Almost all priests who served here came from Europe, and the United States sent no missionaries to other lands. That, however, would change in the early twentieth century because of the vision of two men: Thomas Frederick Price and James Anthony Walsh. On this World Mission Sunday, I will speak only about Fr. Price, a man from our own St. Mary Parish neighborhood.

Thomas Frederick Price, known as "Freddie" to his friends, was born in Wilmington, North Carolina on August 19, 1860, the eighth child of Alfred and Clarissa Bond.

Freddie's parents, who had converted to the Catholic Faith, raised him as Catholic, and the priests of his parish, St. Thomas on Dock Street, influenced him.

One priest, in particular, was influential in Freddie's life; that was James Gibbons, who would eventually become Cardinal Gibbons of Baltimore. On June 20, 1886, Freddie was ordained at St. Thomas Church, becoming the first priest ordained in North Carolina, which at that time was part of the Diocese of Charleston, South Carolina.

As a parish priest, Fr. Price served the people of Asheville and New Bern. Then he received permission to be a traveling evangelist throughout the state. As an evangelist, in 1897 Fr. Price founded a magazine called *Truth*, and in 1898 he established an orphanage in Raleigh called Nazareth. In 1902 he opened a missionary training center in Raleigh to train seminarians to work in home missions—missions in the United States of America.

As time went on, though, Fr. Price began to dream that one day, the Catholic Church in the United States would be strong and mature enough to send American missionaries to other lands. He dreamt of a

210

new missionary religious community to accomplish this task. At the same time, another man—Fr. James Anthony Walsh—had the same dream. When the two got together at a conference they attended, they designed a new order called the Catholic Foreign Mission Society of America, more commonly called Maryknoll. St. Pope Pius X approved the order, and Fr. Price led the first group of Maryknoll missionary priests to China in 1918.

Because of his age, Fr. Price had difficulty learning Chinese, and he suffered from physical ailments. He died on September 12, 1919 in Hong Kong from a burst appendix. His body is buried in the Seminary Chapel at Maryknoll, New York.

Today Maryknoll priests, Brothers, Sisters, and Lay Missionaries serve in nations all over the world including Mexico, and countries of Central America, South America, Asia, and Africa. A lay organization, called Maryknoll Affiliates, commit to praying for missionaries and do limited work in the United States and overseas. In our parish, we have a Spanish-speaking Maryknoll Affiliate Chapter that serves the homeless and poor of Wilmington, N.C.

Today the little boy from Wilmington, N.C. who grew up to be the co-founder of Maryknoll and became known as "The Tar Heel Apostle," is now called Servant of God Thomas Frederick Price. This title means he is officially on his way to sainthood.

Though Americans still send missionaries to other lands, the amount of work they face is more and more staggering. In many parts of the world, priests are responsible for up to one hundred thousand Catholic Christians spread out in many remote areas. As the number of priests in the world decreases, the average age of priests increases. In many parts of the world, the Catholic Church is experiencing what has been called "The Vanishing Eucharist" because the Eucharist is only celebrated once or twice a year.

Despite all odds, there are valiant men and women who continue to serve on the front lines in mission lands. They are the priests, Brothers, Sisters, deacons, and lay missionaries representing you and me. On this World Mission Sunday, please support these heroes who serve in our place.

And that is the good news I have for you on this World Mission Sunday, the Twenty-Ninth Sunday in Ordinary Time.

Story sources:

- John C. Murrett, *Tar Heel Apostle: Thomas Frederick Price: Co-founder of Maryknoll, Catholic Foreign Mission Society of America*, 1944. [Reprinted by Kessinger Publications, 2005.]
- Fr. James F. Garneau, "Father Thomas F. Price: North Carolina's Apostle to the World," *NC Catholics*, Jan/Feb, 2011, pp. 16-19.

Chapter 53

30th Sunday in Ordinary Time – B

Priest Flaws

Scripture:

- Jeremiah 31: 7-9
- Psalm 126: 1-2ab, 2cd-3, 4-5, 6
- Hebrews 5: 1-6
- Mark 10: 46-52

Today Catholic Christians celebrate the Thirtieth Sunday in Ordinary Time. And this year, we celebrate this as Priesthood Sunday, a day we remember ordained priests of our Church.

In today's selection from the Gospel, Jesus tells his disciples that to be a good leader of his people, one must adopt the servant-leadership model. Specifically he said, "Rather, whoever wishes to be great among you will be your servant; whoever wishes to be first among you will be the slave to all" (Mark 10: 43-44).

Sometimes priests do live up to the servant-leadership model that Jesus taught, but sometimes they fail, putting their needs and desires before those of their flock. That is particularly tempting, I believe for those whom I call "ladder climbers," those who want special honors bestowed on them.

Unfortunately, many people think that ordained priests—in contrast to all baptized persons who are part of the "priesthood of all believers"—ought to be above human frailties. Priests, however, have many frailties.

Look at the Apostles handpicked by God the Son, Jesus Christ. These men all had problems—pride, jealousy, anger, cowardice, despair, and even treachery. Nevertheless, out of all the people who ever lived, these are the men Jesus Christ himself chose. Why, then, would we believe that Church leaders today would have a better track record than the ones Jesus chose?

The first time I realized that priests could have human problems was in my late teen years. I was an orderly at St. Thomas Hospital in Akron, Ohio a year before entering nursing school. One evening, one of the Sisters asked if I would stay with a priest who had just been admitted to an alcoholism treatment unit of the hospital. He was very intoxicated and not thinking rationally. Further, the Sister was afraid he would harm himself if left alone. Naturally I agreed.

Little did I know that this hospital unit was destined to become very famous, for it was the first Alcoholics Anonymous-based hospital unit in history. This was the ministry founded by the co-founder of A.A., Dr. Bob Smith, and supported by Sister Ignatia of A.A. fame. At that time, the Sisters of Charity of St. Augustine – of which Sr. Ignatia was part - ran St. Thomas Hospital.

I can still remember the bewilderment I felt that night. How could a priest be drunk? After all, it had been my dream to be an ordained priest since I was four or five years of age. How could a man who had achieved my dream be brought down by alcohol? I had much to learn.

Many years passed, and I was finally a seminarian myself. Now in case you don't know, seminarians can be some of the planet's harshest critics of ordained priests. They see themselves as the ultimate experts on "good" and "bad" priests. But one evening, as one of a group of seminarians sitting around with the Bishop of Cleveland, I heard something that made me stop and think. During our conversation, he said something to the effect that, "Gentlemen, before you pass judgment on a priest, just remember that you have not spent even one day of your lives as a priest. Just remember that: not even one day have you spent as a priest."

Needless to say, that was not something we "experts" wanted to hear. However, it was true. It was absolutely true. Not one of us had spent even one day of our life as an ordained Catholic priest.

Since those seminary days, I have learned much about ordained priests and their problems. Priests can experience the same life problems that others experience, problems such as depression, alcoholism and other forms of addiction, credit card debt, materialism, laziness, procrastination, gossip, stinginess and greed, discouragement, impatience, and a lack of compassion, sensitivity and charity.

In addition to the problems everyone else faces, priests are also more likely to get on "power trips," when some in their flock put them on pedestals and treat them as super-human. These folks come to believe that they indeed are a "cut above" the rest of humanity. They may forget that they are to serve, not be served. They may forget Jesus' washing the feet of his disciples to show a new model of leadership. They may begin to live lifestyles full of privileges denied to ordinary people, privileges such as housekeepers and cooks and free restaurant dinners and free vacations. Some may even turn to morally abhorrent behavior.

But despite the notable flaws of a few ordained priests, I sincerely think most priests, however flawed, want to be holy. They want to be good. They genuinely love to help people in need. They want to give their lives to a greater purpose. They thoroughly enjoy being needed and their lives of service.

On Priesthood Sunday, the Church simply reminds us that ordained priests, like everyone, need prayers and support. That is a call to each and every one of us.

And that is the good news I have for you on this Thirtieth Sunday in Ordinary Time.

Chapter 54

31st Sunday in Ordinary Time – B

The Cobbler's Boots

Scripture:

- Deuteronomy 6: 2-6
- Psalm 18: 2-3a, 3bc-4, 47 and 51ab
- Hebrews 7: 23-28
- Mark 12: 28b-34

Today Catholic Christians celebrate the Thirty-First Sunday in Ordinary Time.

In today's selection from the book of Deuteronomy, we read, "Therefore, you shall love the Lord, your God, with all your heart, and with all your soul, and with all your strength" (Deut. 6: 5).

Then, in the Gospel selection we have from Mark, we hear how a Scribe asked Jesus what the greatest commandment was. Jesus replied, "The first is this: Hear, O Israel! The Lord our God is Lord alone! You shall love the Lord your God with all your heart, with all your soul, with all your mind, and with all your strength. The second is this: You shall love your neighbor as yourself. There is no greater commandment than these" (Mark 12: 29-31).

Through the ages, many people – including preachers of the Word who should know better – have looked at these words of Jesus and come to an incomplete conclusion. They think that just because Jesus so plainly divulged the greatest commandments, that only two commandments form the basis of our faith. What they miss, however, is the third part of the commandment – "yourself." Thus, the great commandment is actually a triple love commandment; we are to love God, neighbor, and self.

In this homily, we look at this third and often neglected part of the triple love commandment – the love of self.

Before examining some Biblical principles that we should take away from the Scriptures, however, let's look at the following story called "The Cobbler's Boots."

There was once a village cobbler who was very busy. Everyone in the village relied on him to fix their shoes and boots and sandals.

One day, the cobbler noticed that his boots were pinching him a bit. But he didn't mind a little discomfort, for after all, he was too busy to stop and repair his own boots.

This wasn't a problem at first, for he was used to being tough and making sacrifices for others. Unfortunately, as time passed, his boots began to deteriorate and fall apart. Soon, while he worked feverishly on others' boots and shoes and sandals, his feet developed blisters. Before he knew it, he even began to limp wherever he went.

218

His customers, noticing his limp, began to worry about the cobbler's health. He reassured them, however, that everything was all right and that they should not worry about him.

However, after a few years, the cobbler's feet got so bad that he had to give up his work and close his shop.

Because he had been the only cobbler in the village, everyone in town soon started to limp in pain as their own shoes, boots, and sandals deteriorated.

All of this pain could be directly traced to the cobbler, who did not take care of himself because he was too busy taking care of everyone else.

Most likely no one in our parish community is a cobbler – or shoemaker. However, the story of the cobbler's boots is not really about boots or cobblers. Rather, it is about what happens when we forget to love and respect our very self. I would imagine that most adults are guilty of not caring for self adequately at some time in their lives, so this Scripture passage and homily is for pretty much everyone who has lived to adulthood. Here are two Biblical principles we can glean from the Scripture and story of the day.

First, love of self is most assuredly the third part of the triple love command of Jesus. When Jesus implored us to love our neighbor, he added that we must do so as we love ourselves. That implies, I think everyone would agree, that we must love ourselves.

Second, love of self involves caring for our physical, mental, and spiritual health. In the realm of physical health, that means we get regular physical checkups, take medications and other forms of physical treatment as prescribed, keep our weight within normal limits, get regular exercise, live prudently, and the like.

Caring for our mental health involves meeting our adult social roles well, being gentle with ourselves, and being glad to be part of the universe. Caring for our mental health means having nurturing friendships and interests that nurture our spirits.

And caring for our spiritual health means we communicate regularly with God in prayer, celebrate the sacraments regularly, participate in parish life, engage in spiritual reading (especially the Bible), and practice corporal and spiritual works of mercy.

If we don't care for ourselves, we can become victims of burnout in our lives. Burnout can happen in our occupations and in our home lives. Signs and symptoms of burnout include frequent exhaustion, lack of joy in daily activities, sleep problems, inability to stop thinking about work, cynicism, taking "sick days" from work when not really sick, failing to take vacations, poor job performance, and the like.

As we continue our life journeys this week, it would be a good idea to reflect on how well we show love of self.

And that is the good news I have for you on this Thirty-First Sunday in Ordinary Time.

Story source: Anonymous, "The Cobbler's Boots," Betterlifecoachingblog.com.

Chapter 55

32nd Sunday in Ordinary Time – B

Grains of Caring

<u>Scripture:</u>

- 1 Kings 17: 10-16
- Psalm 146: 6c-7, 8-9a, 9bc-10
- Hebrews 9: 24-28
- Mark 12: 38-44

Today Catholic Christians celebrate the Thirty-Second Sunday in Ordinary Time.

On this day, we hear two very interesting stories about generosity, one involving a widow in the First Book of Kings and the other involving a poor widow who gave her all to the Lord. In both stories, the widows gave with all their hearts. And in both stories, they both received a very nice reward.

Generosity of time, talent, and/or treasure follows a certain "law of the universe," so to speak: the more we give, the more we get. In the following story, we hear about two brothers who gave from their hearts and received an extremely precious reward.

Once there were two brothers who worked together on the family farm. One was married and had a big family, while the other brother was single. At the end of each day, they shared the produce and profits equally with each other and then went to their own homes.

One night, the brother who was single said to himself, "It does not seem right to me that we should share the produce and the profits equally. After all, I'm alone and my needs are simple. I don't need as much as my brother does." So, every night, he took a sack of grain from his bin and crept across the field between their houses, and dumped the sack of grain into his brother's bin.

Meanwhile, another night, the brother with the large family said to himself, "It's not right that my brother and I share the produce and profit equally. After all, I'm married. I have a wife and children, and they can look after me for years to come. My brother, however, has no one to take care of him in the future." So each night, he took a sack of grain and dumped it into his single brother's bin.

For many years, each of the brothers was puzzled, for their supplies of grain never got smaller. Then, one dark night, the two brothers bumped into each other while running these nightly errands. Slowly, it dawned on them what was happening. They dropped their sacks, embraced one another and became much closer to each other from that day onward.

Now let's look at the two Scripture stories about generosity.

In the Old Testament reading, the Prophet Elijah asked a widow to get him something to eat and drink. She explained to Elijah that she only had enough food for herself and her son, and after they had eaten, she would have nothing left. Then, she said, she and her son would die.

Elijah, however, told her not to worry. So, she fed Elijah, and as a result, she and her son were rewarded with plentiful food for a year.

In the Gospel reading, we hear the famous story of the poor widow, who gave all she had to the Lord, unlike the Scribes, who gave from their surplus. Jesus rewarded her by praising her generosity.

From the story of the two brothers and the Bible stories of today, we can glean these three points about the virtue of generosity.

First, to practice generosity is a Christian commandment. In many places in the Gospels, Jesus tells us that we are to give to our brothers and sisters in need. He gives specific examples such giving drink to the thirsty, consolation to those in mourning, and food to the hungry. He further told us that at the end of time, we would be judged on how we served him by serving others.

Second, generosity should become second nature to us. In other words, our first inclination to those in need should be generosity. Our desire to help others should not be something we have to think deeply about. A few months ago, I saw this principle in action. As they often do, our young Hispanic adult group came to my house for pizza after we our monthly evening Mass. At the end of the evening, one of the members of the group came in late and said, "I need $100." Immediately, everyone who was in hearing distance reached into their pockets to see what they could come up with. Absolutely no one asked what the young man needed the money for. It was not important to them. What was important was that a brother needed money, and together they met his need. I can't tell you what a blessing such an examples is for a pastor.

There are also times when "no" is a better response. That, however, is for another day, another homily.

Third, our generosity will bring rewards. For the two farm brothers, generosity brought renewed love. For the Old Testament widow, it brought sufficient food for a year. And for the New Testament widow, it brought praise from God the Son. I can't tell you how many times I hear stories of amazement from people who give to others and then find God showering them with both material and spiritual blessings.

As we continue our life journeys this week, it would be good to reflect on our own generosity by asking ourselves, "How generous am I?"

And that is the good news I have for you on this Thirty-Second Sunday in Ordinary Time.

Story source: Anonymous, "Grains of Caring," in Brian Cavanaugh's *Sower's Seeds That Nurture Family Values: Sixth Planting*, New York: Paulist Press, 2000, #51, pp. 59-60.

Chapter 56

33rd Sunday in Ordinary Time – B

A Shack in Heaven

<u>Scripture:</u>

- Daniel 12: 1-3
- Psalm 16: 5 & 8, 9-10, 11
- Hebrews 10: 11-14, 18
- Mark 13: 24-32

Today Catholic Christians celebrate the Thirty-Third Sunday in Ordinary Time.

On this day, we are faced with readings about the end of the world. In the reading from Daniel, for example, we hear about how some souls will live forever, while others will suffer in horror and disgrace. And in the Gospel, we hear about the end of the world, when God will send angels to "gather his elect from the four winds, from the end of the earth to the end of the sky."

The Church has chosen apocalyptic Bible passages for this Sunday because the Church Year will be coming to a close in just two weeks. Year B, the Year of Mark, will end, and we will begin Year C, the Year of Luke.

When we think about the end of time, it's natural to think of what will happen to us when we die. As Catholic Christians, we not only hope for heaven for ourselves, but we pray every day for the salvation of all human beings.

Sometimes, when we reflect on heaven, we pay insufficient attention to how our actions on Earth may impact our experience afterwards. That is exactly what happened to the woman in the following half-serious, half-joking story told by Winifred Eastment.

There was once a woman who lived in a magnificent mansion surrounded by a beautifully landscaped garden. She was very much in love with all the finer things of life. She loved to buy herself expensive clothes, jewelry, cars, boats, furniture, paintings, vacations, and every other thing that "tickled her fancy." Unfortunately, the woman never thought of sharing her good fortune with others, for she was always afraid that if she gave to others, there would not be enough for herself.

Her faithful old gardener, however, approached life totally differently. Though he was very poor, he saw the world as a wonderful place, filled with beautiful, simple things. He marveled at the wonders God had created—the flowers and trees he cared for, the birds that sang as he worked in the gardens, butterflies, the interesting shapes of the clouds, and the stars and moon of the nighttime skies. From the little amount of money he made, he was always ready to help those in need.

One day, the woman died and went to heaven. St. Peter walked her down incredible streets made of gold, past beautiful mansions.

226

Finally, they came to a very run-down shack. "This is your eternal home," replied St. Peter.

"Oh, there must be a mistake. I am used to real quality. I am used to having everything that money can buy. I can't possibly live in that rundown shack!"

Then, the woman spotted a magnificent mansion being built nearby and said, "How about that place! That is exactly what I want."

St. Peter said, "I'm sorry, Ma'am, but you can't have the magnificent mansion. We are getting that ready for your gardener when he comes."

The woman exclaimed, "My gardener? But he is used to living in a tiny cottage! Why couldn't you give him the shack and me the mansion?"

St. Peter said, "I'm very sorry, Ma'am, it's out of my hands. We can only build with the materials you sent up to us when you lived on Earth. Your gardener always sent up magnificent material. You, though, have sent up sub-standard material. In fact, it's a miracle you even got a shack!"

What can we make of such an anecdote? Here are three things that come to mind when I think about the materialistic woman and her heavenly shack.

First, such stories are not meant to give us the idea that we can "earn" heaven, or even a better "home" in heaven. Salvation, in the Catholic Christian view, is a gift from God. Gifts are freely given; salaries are earned. It is the giver who decides to give the gift, not the person who receives it. Catholic Christians believe God can give this gift to anyone he chooses to give it to. That is why we pray each day for God to give the gift of eternal salvation to every human being who ever lived, who is alive today, and who ever will live. We do this because we believe in God's infinite love and mercy, and because we believe that "With God, all things are possible."

Second, though we believe we don't "earn" salvation, Jesus has given us various stories about how our behavior on Earth can determine how great our reward will be in the afterlife. I remember when I was a child, the Religious Sisters who were my teachers would often call good deeds the "stars in your crown." The idea was that the more "stars" in our crown, the better off we'd be in heaven. To my knowledge, though,

227

I don't think that ever was an official Catholic teaching, but more of a pious folk belief.

Third, now on Earth is the time to follow Christ with all our hearts. Now is the time to show our love of Christ as he lives in our brothers and sisters in need. Now is the time to put into practice what Jesus taught us. When we die, our chance to do these things comes to an end. My paternal grandmother used to say, "Make hay while the sun shines." Our life on Earth is the time of the shining sun.

As we continue our life journeys this week, it might be good to reflect on what kind of building materials we are sending up to heaven for the construction of our heavenly homes. Are we building a shack or a mansion?

And that is the good news I have for you on this Thirty-Third Sunday in Ordinary Time.

Story source: Winifred Eastment, "The Shack in Heaven," in Anthony Castle (Ed.), *A Treasury of Quips, Quotes, & Anecdotes for Preachers and Teachers*, Mystic, CT: Twenty-Third Publications, 1998, pp. 125-126.

Chapter 57

Christ the King – B

The Dog and the Moon

Scripture:

- Daniel 7: 13-14
- Psalm 93: 1ab, 1c-2, 5
- Revelation 1: 5-8
- John 18: 33b-37

Today Catholic Christians celebrate the last Sunday of the Church Year. This past year, we have been in Cycle B, the Year of St. Mark. That means that most of the Gospel readings we had was from Mark's Gospel. Next Sunday, we begin Year C, the Year of St. Luke.

A "church" or "liturgical" year may be seen as one long story, a story taking us from the foretelling of the coming of a Messiah to his birth and his life and his death and his resurrection and his ascension. But like every story, there should be an end.

Because Catholic Christianity has a profound romantic theme, our endings are filled with joy. That is why the Church, for the last Sunday of the church year, celebrates the Feast of Christ the King. On this day, we tell the end of the story: good will triumph over evil, and peace will triumph over chaos. In the Catholic Christian view, the end is not in doubt.

But though Catholic Christians believe that good will triumph over evil, we know that the journey towards the glorious end is fraught with dangers we must endure. And before we think we should be immune to such dangers, all we have to do is look at the life of Christ to see that not even God the Son was immune from sorrow. Jesus was, in fact, tortured and suffered the death penalty. If Jesus had to suffer, why would we think we should somehow be immune?

Sometimes, though, we become so concerned about the problems we face, that we become distracted or fearful or unsure of ourselves. Take, for example, religious leaders. Sometimes, when religious leaders proclaim the good news of Jesus, they are assaulted by contrary voices. Often these voices are members of their own flock. And when the contrary voices become too shrill or hostile, it takes a strong leader to step back, reflect, and then come to the realization that truth does not change; only people change.

That is what we see in the following story that I call "The dog and the moon."

There was once a politician who did the very best job he could. However, because he was a human, he sometimes made mistakes along the way. When he made a mistake, critics attacked him. Reporters, for example, would repeat his errors in their newspapers.

One day, when the criticism got to him, the politician decided to get out of town and visit his dear friend, a farmer. "What am I to do?" exclaimed the politician. "I try so hard. Nobody has tried harder than I have to do good for people, and yet I get so much criticism!"

The old farmer, however, could not hear the politician's complaint too well because his dog was barking loudly at the full moon. The farmer told the dog to be quiet, but the dog just kept on howling at the moon. Finally, the old famer turned to the politician and said, "Do you want to know how you should handle your unfair critics? Here's how. Listen to that dog; now look up at the moon. And remember that people will keep criticizing you. They'll keep nipping at your heels. But remember this lesson: The dog keeps howling, but the moon keeps shining."

This is a very powerful lesson for religious leaders to learn. There will always be people criticizing them for one reason or another. The important thing, though, is that the leader keeps presenting the good news of Jesus Christ by his or her life example and by his or her preaching.

As the critics call for exclusion, leaders must preach inclusion.

As critics advocate vengeance, leaders must preach forgiveness.

As critics call for hate, leaders must preach love.

As critics yell for prejudice, leaders must preach acceptance.

As critics present in an angry and hostile fashion, leaders must preach their message with joy and good will.

But the message of Christ the King does not just refer to religious leaders. On the contrary, the message of the final good triumphing over evil is a message for all Christians.

All Christians, by virtue of their baptism, are part of the "priesthood of all believers." As priests, they are called to consistently follow the triple love command of Jesus Christ. They are called to shine like the moon, not be like a pack of dogs howling at the moon.

As we continue our life journeys this week, it would be a good idea to take some time to ask ourselves some questions such as: How do I show love consistently in my life? Am I more like a light in the world or more like an angry critic of those who try to shine Christ's light in the dark places of our world?

And that is the good news I have for you on this last Sunday of the Church Year, the Feast of Christ the King.

Story source: Anonymous, "Handling criticism," in Brian Cavanaugh (Ed.), *The Sower's Seeds,* New York: Paulist Press, 1990, # 64, p. 52.

Made in the USA
Middletown, DE
14 October 2023